ONE BOY'S WAR

To Rex
With the author's best wishes

David

ONE BOY'S WAR

DAVID FINDLAY CLARK

First published 1997

Aberdeenshire Council
Leisure and Recreation

© David Findlay Clark

ISBN : 1 901 275 02 7

Printed and bound in Scotland by
BPC - AUP Aberdeen Ltd.

Acknowledgments

The author would like to thank the "Banffshire Journal" for allowing the extracts from its pages to be used in this publication and to acknowledge gratefully the agreement of Ian Cook, photographer, Greenwich and Saga Publishing Ltd, Folkestone to the use of the illustration on the front cover, for which Mr Cook holds copyright. He is also indebted to Robin Donnelly and Anne Meldrum for contributions from their memories of certain incidents and to Forbes Law for help in sourcing some of the illustrations. Thanks are also due to Jim Hughes and Benevenagh Books, author and publishers of "A Steep Turn to the Stars" for their permission to use a number of illustrations from that publication and to Chaz Bowyer for permission to use the photograph on p 97.

He would also like to thank Iain Macaulay, formerly Senior Arts Development Officer, Aberdeenshire Council, for his help in preparing the typescript for publication and Murray Webster of BPC-AUP for helpful advice and discussion prior to printing.

Any errors or omissions there may be elsewhere in the body of the text are the responsibility of the author alone and must be seen as the product of the caprice of memory.

Dedication

To my four delightful grandchildren,
Scotty, Cameron, Kerr and Kirsty.

May they know in their lifetimes
only peace and happiness.

FOREWORD

Just over fifty years since World War 2 came to an end, it is apparent that much of the first-hand observation of these trying times has been recorded. There is a wealth of information about the hazards of combat on land, in the air and on the sea. Much has been written about the impact of war on the ordinary citizenry of our country and of all the others caught up in the conflagration. Official histories of several kinds and retrospective analyses of the events and exigencies of the war have emerged in a steady stream since 1945. There is much less, however, written from the point of view of a child of those times who was just not quite old enough to be called up to fight (although, oddly now it will seem, he was all too keen to do so at the time) but old enough for the events and experiences of growing up in a war-torn country to have made some impact on his consciousness.

There were hardships and times to be frightened, but there were excitements and adventures too. Some memories are necessarily lost forever - some too harsh, most perhaps too trivial - but others remain indelibly cast on the *tabula rasa* of a young mind. Accepting the capriciousness of recall after all these years, the writer has tried to capture something of the flavour both of boyishness in straitened circumstances and of growing up in a period of great uncertainty, when the solemnity, sometimes the humour and occasionally the stress forced one into a premature adulthood. It was a time when the normal travails of adolescence, allegedly a period of *Sturm und Drang* in itself, were submerged in daily events which we now recognise as of huge historical significance but which then were simply the stuff of life and part of the daily round. But they were formative days nonetheless and it has seemed worthwhile to give this record a chance to become part of the vernacular history of North East Scotland.

CONTENTS

"People are trapped in history
and history is trapped in them"

James Baldwin, "Stranger in the Village" (1953)

Forsan et haec olim meminisse iuvabit

(Virgil, "Aeneid" 1 : 1

(Perhaps even these things will someday be pleasant to remember)

CHAPTER 1

DECLARATION

"Fours don't hold hands!" cried my young grandson indignantly to his Grannie one day when he was just that age. He, maturing rapidly, had just been collected from the nursery school and was agog with new information about feeding the goldfish; about painting with glue mixed in with his colours; and with the latest in social mores for the pre-school child. His little declaration reminded me that neither did nines cry in church.

It took me back abruptly to that grey, blustery morning in September 1939 when I walked home from the Parish kirk in Banff with my brother, desultorily kicking at the fallen leaves. I hoped that he had not seen, three quarters of an hour previously, the few tears that had unaccountably appeared in the corners of my eyes. Then, the whole congregation, hushed and apprehensive, listened to Mr Chamberlain, his voice thready and distorted, partly by atmospherics and partly by emotion, declare that Germany had invaded Poland and in consequence Britain had declared war on Germany. The language he used for a matter of such heavy significance was strangely prosaic without any of the sonorous resonances with which Winston Churchill was later to imbue his every word to the nation. "This morning, the British ambassador in Berlin handed the German government a final note stating that unless we heard from them by 11o'clock that they were prepared at once to withdraw their troops from Poland, a state of war would exist between us. I have to tell you now that no such undertaking has been received and that consequently this country is at war with Germany."

Unaware that the adult world, or at least the more perceptive part of it, had for the best part of a year anticipated terrible things at the hands of Adolf Hitler, in my childish way I fully expected, following the sudden declaration, sudden events. It slightly surprised me that straight away the sky had not become black with diving Stukas, each ruthless and determined Nazi pilot fully committed to the

1

annihilation of Banff and all its citizens - especially me. Such is the guilt intrinsic to an upbringing in the near Calvinistic rectitude and order of a Scottish manse!

As it happens, I was not alone in sensing the terrible portent of that hour in the church on the 3rd of September 1939. There may well have been so much communicated emotion then that I could hardly claim any special sensitivity to the situation as the cause of my tears. The "Banffshire Journal" of 5th September 1939 described the episode thus:

> "In the community of Banff the news of the declaration of war, notwithstanding that it had been expected, caused, when it swiftly came in the end, a profound impression and the sense of gravity that descended on every home and individual with the Prime Minister's fateful and emotional broadcast announcement was certainly not relieved by the desolate weather conditions experienced locally at the time. The violent storm of wind and lashing rain that arose vividly gave the impression that all Nature was outraged by the folly of mankind, and that the very heavens had angered and wept. And a strange coincidence was that on the very stroke of eleven o'clock, at which the unsatisfied British ultimatum to Germany expired, a vivid flash of lightning rent the dark skies and was followed at once by a startling crack of thunder. Then the gale blew its greatest fury, and torrential rain lashed the countryside. In the tragic circumstances of the moment it was a coincidence that touched the imagination of many people on this fateful and historically sombre Sunday morning. A warning had come on the morning news service at ten o'clock of the grave import of the message to be received from the Premier's lips at eleven fifteen, and in these circumstances, together with those of the terrific rainstorm then reaching its climax, fewer people than usual left home to attend the church services at eleven o'clock.

DECLARATION

In view of the gravity of the occasion, hurried arrangements were made to have portable wireless receivers placed in both St Mary's and Trinity churches, so that the congregations would hear the Prime Minister's words. At St. Mary's the usual service was departed from on account of the momentous event. After the minister, Rev. D Findlay Clark (my father), had led in prayer of intercession, the wireless set, placed on the Communion table, was turned on, and with bowed heads the congregation listened to Mr Chamberlain's solemn statement. On his deeply emotional final words being uttered - "Now, may God bless you all, and may He defend the Right.....", the congregation were visibly affected, and women buried their heads in their hands and wept. At the request of the minister the congregation stood and sang the National Anthem. Mr Clark, speaking with effort, said he felt it would be inopportune and inappropriate for him to add anything to what they had heard. All they could do was to abide by the decision and stand fast - in defence of the liberty whereby we had been made free. The service was then curtailed. The congregation sang the hymn, "Lord, while for all mankind we pray", and Mr Clark pronounced the benediction. Young women went from the church in tears.....

Throughout the day, which remained dull but gradually improved, the sense of the seriousness of the occasion was everywhere manifest in the community, but through all conversation ran the firm note of determination that the task, now taken up, however long and bitter, must be carried to a victorious end."

In retrospect, it is fascinating to observe the somewhat engaging facet of the Nor'east character and habit whereby, even in one of the most momentous moments of history, the Editor could not desist from the link between the weather and the events of the day. The day was "dull, but gradually improved". What a metaphor for the next five years!

3

Not that the declaration had been wholly unexpected by many people in Banff. The newspaper had reported a spirited discussion about the siting of the new high-powered electric air raid warning siren. Even when it was placed, as it was to remain, on top of the gaol, some worthy citizens complained that it could not be heard from indoors. One strong protagonist of its present siting, however, pointed out that the intention of the siren was to warn people to get indoors if they were out rather than out if they were in, so it should be all right where it was. No doubt the prisoners were wakened from their sleep very efficiently, but they were not likely to be going out anywhere anyway.

Additionally, all through August, the townsfolk had seen "The Terriers" gathering, equipping and marching away from the Drill Hall and the Plainstones in the centre of the town. Smart, erect and impressive they all were too - the postie, a carpenter, builders' labourers, a photographer, bakers, electricians, and some less well kent faces from the country, all fully kitted and shouldering their Lee-Enfield .303's and here and there, a Bren gun. Many were to be taken prisoner at and around St. Valery and Dunkirk and some were to be mourned and their names read later from the granite memorial "To Our Glorious Dead" at the foot of Seafield Street.

A year earlier, my brother Tom and I had been roused from our beds at the, for us, late hour of 10:30pm or thereabouts. Father had a serious expression and gave us to understand that we were about to listen to a moment of history. Minister and erstwhile schoolteacher, he had always had a fine sense of the dramatic - and a penchant for the stage for which the pulpit had often been a surrogate. We, in our dressing gowns and bare feet, pandered to this by assuming expressions that could have been taken by the naive to be solemn but were more likely to have been the wide-eyed vacuousness of simple puzzlement. We were about to hear the so-called "Peace in our time" statement of Neville Chamberlain as he climbed from the airliner that had just taken him back from his appeasement meeting with Herr Hitler in Munich. At the end of it my father simply shook his head. "It's no good. This is simply a postponement." We were not fully apprised of the true significance of the moment, but were somewhat more likely to believe our father than Mr Chamberlain.

It is doubtful whether our notions of what war might involve

DECLARATION

had developed in any significant way over the course of that past year. Perhaps it was something my parents had discussed in hushed tones in the privacy of my father's study. Certainly other small boys with whom we mixed seemed remarkably unchastened by the prospect. Up till that time, war had been equated in our heads with deploying numbers of lead toy soldiers, a few tanks and Dinky toy field guns in tactically secure positions behind chairlegs on the parlour floor, while various other model Indians or Legionnaires were positioned on the battlements of a plywood fort still usable after several Christmasses. It is certain that at least the more perceptive of the adults around the town were well aware of the sense of tension throughout Europe in the months preceeding the declaration but even officialdom seemed to awaken to its responsibilities only with some reluctance and there was little to show for such a delayed awakening in the form of military activity locally until a very few days in the late August of 1939.

Had we but known, the holocaust to come was then being presaged by ominous signs of antisemitism. The local press had told only nine months before the war's beginning that there was on sale in Germany a brand new board game called "Out with Jews".This was to be played with little non-Aryan figures which could be moved around the board at the throw of a dice as each player attempted to get his Jews from Germany to Palestine. The manufacturers stated that the game was "tastefully produced and strongly made" and would soon be a "quick selling line in all toyshops"

On that night, however, we crowded round the quaint curved and polished walnut of the Art Deco wireless, its one and a half inch wide tuning dial with the mysterious numbers glowing orange in the gas light. It was a Murphy and had two batteries, a wet and a dry one. The latter was terribly expensive but fortunately seemed to last quite a long time if we rationed our listening to "The News", some Scottish dance music and "Children's Hour". That battery stored 120 volts. At the time that to me seemed very powerful. The "wet" battery, however, had become less formidable by dint of my closer acquaintanceship with it as I frequently was the one chosen to take it, being careful not to drop it or spill the acid, to Harry Watson's, the electrical shop, for charging. It carried, like me, fewer volts than the dry battery, but being of glass, it did show its lead plates and acid level just below the metal strap of the simple handle used to carry it. At least its physical properties were open to examination and wonderment - not like the other one, all hidden zinc and chemicals behind a cover of waxed paper. One of the town's less sophisticated   souls was heard to berate her bairn for being careless with the wet battery one day. "Haud that thing still on yer waey doon tae Watson's, ye vratch, or ye'll reeshle up a' the stations!"

Just over a year later, having graduated to Secondary education at Banff Academy, I was to be initiated into the deeper mysteries of electronics by the local AA man, in whose house one of my school pals, a refugee with an Austrian civil engineer father and a Hungarian doctor mother, rented rooms. This skilled and friendly man looked with genial tolerance on the 'cat's whisker' and quartz crystal I was then using to listen secretly to William Joyce, Lord Haw Haw, the traitor who broadcast from Germany daily on long wave. Away from his motor bike and yellow and black sidecar, Mr Scholes, our radio mentor, had an old wooden box or drawer full of mightily intriguing bits and pieces. There were some simple thermionic valves, a variety of dusty, and, by today's standards, large   resistors and condensers and, even more intriguing, some variable condensers with their dull aluminium blades just waiting to be rotated to see whether there had been any breakdown in the airspace insulation between them. It was hard for us to keep our hands out of that box.

Part of the motivation for our enthusiasm about the quartz crystal and cat's whisker derived from the fact that such an apparatus did not require a battery. We could not have afforded that. As it was, my parents exercised a fairly strict control over wireless listening time, partly so that it would not interfere with my homework for school and partly because the batteries required for the "proper" wireless were so expensive.

So far as my own little set was concerned, the bedsprings were my aerial and with the aid of a few resistors, one capacitor, a handwound coil on the cardboard former of a toilet roll and a cheap pair of 2000ohm earphones it was possible to monitor his nasal "Germany calling!" preamble and the rest of what we had no doubt were lies about the great and recurrent victories of the Nazis. While my physics master laboured to instil the expansion of metals and gases into the rest of the class, a couple of my pals and I were learning by doing it how to build, first, a one valve receiver with a variable condenser to allow tuning to different stations, and then to add an amplification stage by using a second thermionic valve and a transformer. Money spent on second-hand bits and pieces was saved by not eating sweeties and not buying comics. We did not bother with the administrative details of applying for licences although I am sure that our fiddling with the reactance condensers must from time to time have set the neighbours' wirelesses humming and whistling intolerably. They probably put it down to the Germans!

Looking back to these little adventures in physics leads one to wonder the more at the modern miracles of electronics. Given that war always lends impetus to developments in science, we have seen in the past few decades the development of transistors, semiconductors and now integrated circuits. If we watched with some ignorance the erection of strange aerial arrays on the coast and later wondered at the developments which enabled our aircraft to find surfaced enemy U-boats with almost unerring accuracy and to bomb targets hidden by cloud, we were in a couple of years' time to heap adulation on the Brechin man, (later to become Sir) Robert Watson Watt, who had outdone all the others in electronics to invent and develop the principles of radar. Certainly in electronics and to a lesser extent in the other sciences, one sees how, in less than a generation, knowledge and technology have fed upon themselves to grow exponentially - the original Frankenstein monster only just under control.

CHAPTER 2

ANTICIPATIONS

Putting aside for a moment that little digression, sparked off - if you'll forgive the pun - by the story of the battery charging and the home-made wireless, the intervening year between the appeasement speech and the declaration of war had been noteworthy only for the unremitting routine of Primary school disciplines, academic and otherwise. One teacher had already decided that Guardsmanlike briskness and uniformity was to be the order of the day for all of us - especially those whose classrooms were upstairs. She habitually took up station half way up the school staircase (solid concrete) and set up a rhythmic and firm hand clap to set the tempo of our march upstairs. Woe betide any poor laggard or incoordinate who tripped, missed a step or shuffled! One day, a warning; the next, the strap!

Nor was this our only foretaste of military discipline. "The Jannie" (janitor) was a brusque and burly man who had been a Pipe Major of both bravery as a man and distinction as a piper in what we had learned to call The Great War. Few, including the "Reccie" (Rector or Headmaster) failed to defer in matters both temporal and spiritual to him in his wisdom. For after all, was it not he who had the power to allow a boy or a girl to pull the bellrope to end "playtime" or to call the playground shinhackers from their football to the order of the classroom? There were a few creeps who hung around him at the breaks currying favour in the hope of preferment, but the "Jannie" was an even- as well as a heavy-handed man and he was more than capable of discerning who needed the little boost of winning the job and thrilling to the way the recoil of the bellrope lifted the puller into the air before he (girls were never allowed to pull the bellrope) fell back into the crouch position at the depth of the pull.

He wore, with distinction and style, his uniform of peaked cap, blue serge suit with waistcoat from which hung a gold fob cairngorm (smoky quartz) to balance his pocket watch. From the latter, we believed, the school, and probably the Greenwich Observatory, took its time. His bearing was unmistakably military and his short ginger moustache neatly trimmed. His all-seeing eye took in immediately whether a playground fight should be left alone (if a bully was getting his come-uppance) or whether his timely and muscular intervention was required to prevent either physical or psychological damage to the participants. Later, he would decide whether this was something the Rector should know about. Were he to let it pass, such a discretionary silence, of course, placed antagonists immediately in his debt. For some weeks thereafter there would always be some boy available to run errands, help with marking the football pitch or sweep out "the pegs".

Small boys in Primary school, and for some time later, do not believe that teachers or Janitors exist in the same world as the schoolboy laity. Teachers and Janitors never swore, broke wind, got bored with the sameness of things, nor did they have a private life with people around them who saw them simply as human beings.

We could not know that the janitor could while away the hours with pipes or chanter, composing as well as playing and thus leaving as his memorial some fine pipe tunes. He also seemed to have acquired from some unknown source four or five aged but usable long-barrelled flintlock rifles like those we used to see in the old black and white films about the Afghan Wars or the early wild West. The outbreak of war was the signal for him to use these to introduce us to the elements of rifle drill and Army discipline and ritual. The Lifeboys, Scouts or Boys' Brigade may have been all very well for fun on a Friday night, but to make men of us, fit to defend our country to the last, we had to enrol in the Sandyhill Rifles.

Thus it was that my brother and a few of our pals from Sandyhill Road and the neighbouring streets were constrained to drill under the eagle eye and unremitting rigour of "the Jannie" every Saturday morning - first, till we were fit to be seen in public, in the spartan privacy of the old Woodwork Room in the separate part of the school adjoining the Janitor's house, and subsequently, in the street outside. Sadly, that little school and house has long since been demolished and has been replaced by a little garden - truly, a garden of remembrance!

There, we learned the mysterious importance of responding immediately to command - brisk but unflinching - as well as the whole gamut of military drill. The Boys' Brigade in particular, though I was then just in the Lifeboys, its junior arm, had always considered that quasi-military drills and marching was one of the better ways of knocking our superegos into shape. Simple matters we already knew about, like standing to "Attention", "At ease" and "Easy" required no further training. The rifles, however, and some of us then, half their size, and having some difficulty with their 8lb. weight, came into their own as we learned to "Shoulder arms", "Present arms", "Port arms" and stand at ease with a rifle etc. All of these skills were drilled into us at the proper tempo and using the subvocalised "one-pause-two-pause-three" routine that nearly all of us were to find so handy when we were called up for National Service some ten or so years later. After "the Jannie" and the Sandyhill Rifles, RSM Brittain and various other psychopathic Drill Sergeants were gentle nursemaids by comparison.

It is a sobering thought that in this day and age the phenomenon of a middle-aged man drilling five or six schoolboys of tender years on a Saturday morning might have led to social workers investigating his *bona fides* and whether we were children "at risk". My memories contain nothing but events of the utmost propriety and nothing that might have suggested by word or deed that motives other than the best were at work. We eventually became skilled and coordinated enough to be sent off on our own on "route marches", rifles at the slope, bandoliers polished, berets or Balmorals at the slant, carefully in step until the narrowness and overgrown grass and brambles of the "Cruik-n-crashin' roadie" necessitated single file and we became just a trace uncoordinated. By the time we came down Bellevue Road again, however, he was eyeing us from the corner and we dared not show any signs of sloppiness. Sometimes a change of route would have us marching in all solemnity down through the grounds of Duff House. As an Adam designed ex-mansion house of the aristocracy, hotel and sanatorium it remained sufficiently grandiose and isolated among its specimen trees to give us the feeling that we were there on sufferance. Soon, however, we were to be forbidden entry, not by the gentry but by the proper Army in the form of the Pioneer Corps who suddenly descended on the place with diggers, cement mixers, barbed wire and other impedimenta, bent on converting the place to a Prisoner of War Camp.

ANTICIPATIONS

Even then, and it fascinated me to find it again during my "square-bashing" days in the RAF, we were caught up in a strange but powerful need to perform well in the corporate endeavour. Any recalcitrant whose rifle was at the wrong angle or who couldn't keep in step became an object of derision and something near to hate. We never wondered why - either about that, or about why this giant in blue serge should have felt the need to re-create his days of military glory. But, like so many childhood events, it had an inherent transience, and after some months we were disposed to merge our drills and militarism into the perhaps more normal activities of gang warfare between the street gangs in different parts of the town or fights against our traditional boyish enemies, the Macduffers across the bay.

The early months of the war were marked by a series of brief excitements. The first of these was the regular plotting of the battle lines and such petty victories as the Allies enjoyed during these months of the "phoney war". We were a relatively "bookish" household and I was encouraged to read and evaluate the press reports of the war and avidly to listen in to the "News" on the wireless.

The latter, to work properly, required a long copper wire aerial strung between the chimneys at the top of the house, with another copper wire stretching down from one end of it to a carbon rod which took the signal through the window frame in the parlour. Adjacent to that was a single-pole, single-throw switch of copper about 4 inches long on the window sill which we were sternly adjured to open at any sign of a thunderstorm. My father, knowing nothing of the mysteries of physics, but being very strong on the wrath of God, was punctilious in the extreme about this switch. Any distant rumbles or the gloomy proximity of a large cumulo-nimbus and the switch was thrown. No more "Children's Hour" or, later, the "Hot Club de Paris" for me. Father firmly believed that a bolt of lightning strong enough to vaporise the lot of us could be led, were that switch to be closed, into the heart of the Manse, or, equally unlikely, could be forestalled entirely were the switch to be opened.

Nevertheless, on the wallpaper near the wireless I had pinned up a map of the world with a lot of pink on it. I was never sure why pink should have signified the British Empire. The Pinko's of latter-day USA would certainly have had nothing to do with it. On this map I had stuck little paper flags (which came with it as a cheap offer from,

I think, "The Daily Express"). These were either Union jacks or Swastikas and with them I marked what I believed to be the current boundaries of the warring sides. I vividly remember pinning a Union jack to the dot marked Montevideo when the "Graf Spee" was scuttled after a thrilling combat with HMS "Ajax", "Achilles" and "Exeter". I had not had the heart to pin a Swastika in the middle of Scapa Flow when the "Royal Oak" was torpedoed there by a German U-boat. That was in October 1939, a little over a month from my shameful tears in the kirk.

A few years ago I found myself on a steamer sailing the Norwegian Hurtigrute from Bergen to the North Cape and back. Quietly watching the golden magic of the midnight sun near the Lofoten Islands one night I chatted in a mixture of German and English with a young looking man a few years older than myself. He turned out to have been a submariner in the same boat, for a time, as Captain Prien, the bold skipper of that very U-boat which so successfully and so damagingly challenged our defences at Scapa. We were genial, relaxed in each other's company and shared several interests which extended our conversation of total friendliness beyond the trivial. Both of us were striken by the futility of war, even if, at the time, each had seen it to be necessary. Fifty years or more can make such a difference!

With the change of moral climate which came after the war and more especially, after Vietnam, it is hard to grasp just how belligerent and single minded we were in those hard days and for some years thereafter. Today we are shocked and horrified by the sabotage of a Boeing 747 over Lockerbie killing nearly 300. In those days we became hardened to horror when one morning we heard of the loss of HMS "Hood" - thought to be the pride of the navy - with only three survivors of its 1420 crew members. And that was just one morning to be followed by many others.

As the war wore on we became used to the daily lists of those killed in action, missing and wounded in the daily papers, and, nearer home, the list of local lads, similarly classified, posted outside the Townhouse. One of my father's gloomier tasks was to offer such comfort as he could to those parishioners thus bereaved or stricken with the anxiety of uncertainty. Those whose sons or fathers were posted missing would hope against hope that a later message would confirm that they were prisoners of war. If they were in the Royal Navy or Merchant Marine (as many from the north of Scotland were) the chances of survival long enough to be taken prisoner were slim. Nevertheless, one of my current golfing friends, a former gunner on armed merchantmen, survived three minings or torpedoings then and still lives (at the time of writing) to enjoy his golf and his grandchildren.

CHAPTER 3

PREPARATIONS

Another abiding memory of these early days of the war was of the issue of Identity Cards, Ration Books and gas masks. Of the first named, we needed only to carry them with us at all times. The concept of an identity crisis was a luxury to be reserved for later decades of decadence and plenty. We did have to remember our Identity number. If we failed, we lost our identity. These letter and digit combinations assumed an importance far beyond our names. After all, we already took these for granted. Half a century on I can easily repeat SUMN 24/3, just as some years later my RAF 1250 (Service Identity Card) bore the magic number 2536746, equally firmly emblazoned on my heart. As for our Ration Books, we handed over all responsibility to our mothers - with the possible exception of our "sweetie coupons" which allowed us, if we had the cash, to buy a few boiled sweets or a Mars bar every week. The limit of supply then was 4ozs. per person per week. Chewing gum became a reality only after the American entry into the war and especially if you had an older sister!

The gas mask business was, however, altogether more serious. At the beginning of the war, the Air Raid Precautions organisation (ARP) had already been formed in anticipation of another "Blitzkrieg" such as had been visited on Warsaw and was later to hit Rotterdam. The local organisation consisted of a number of Air Raid Wardens who had the responsibility of ensuring that the blackout was rigorously observed, that there was a proper distribution of pails of sand,water and stirrup pumps, that the availability of heavy rescue and First Aid services was known and, not least, that we all possessed gas masks and knew how to wear them, and if need be, work in them. For most of us schoolboys the regular model gas mask was a simple rubber face piece with a one piece celluloid eye visor and the familiar pignose of a cylindrical carbon and fibre filter. The whole unflattering gubbins was held in place by adjustable straps over one's head. The Wardens and the military had much more serious looking jobs with two round glass eyepieces and a concertina structured tube from the face mask to a filter system in a foot square haversack slung over the shoulder or on the chest. Babies were virtually enveloped in a rubber and celluloid cocoon into which the mother had to pump filtered air by a hand bellows. Many must have wondered how long they might have had to continue to pump in the worst of eventualities.

The original distribution and fitting of gas masks was done at school. One afternoon the Warden and the teacher combined to pass around to each child the soon to become familiar buff cardboard box about 8" cubed containing our gas masks. First, we were taught to smear the eyepiece with an anti-misting compound without letting it touch the rubber parts (which it might have degraded rather quickly).

We were to learn later that if you ran out of anti-misting compound, then a good smear of saliva would do the trick! Then we were to insert the chin into the lower part of the mask and pull the straps over the top of the head, adjusting them so that the mask would fit closely and firmly around the face but not so tightly as to asphyxiate us. As we exhaled, the exhausted air was meant to escape past the edges at our cheeks. The boys were quick to discover in class that a vigorous exhalation caused the mask to vibrate like a "whoopsy cushion" and a few less responsible souls would take the chance to break wind noisily while this performance was in train. We did not take the threat of being gassed too seriously. Any child able to survive attending the outside toilets at the back of the school considered himself immune to the Germans' worst assaults.

Smells were an intrinsic part of school life then. The rubber of the masks was characteristic and unforgettable - like the sweetish, pungent and mildly romantic smell of aircraft fabric, the volatile and aromatic dope that was painted on that fabric, machine oil and fuel of which every hangar and every plane was redolent in my days in the RAF. Even chalk and the hard-backed blackboard dusters, sometimes used as missiles by the teachers, had a special chalk dust smell. Most of the boys then wore tweed shorts and corduroy jerkins which, when wet with snow or rain, or worse, emitted another odour as real to us as that of the dubbin we had to rub into the school footballs and our boots. Scatological quips and jokes abounded although swearing was heard very much less than nowadays and I remember vividly once being careless enough to describe my brother, I think, as a "cheeky little bugger" within the hearing of my mother. That warranted an immediate calling in to be walloped and lectured to by my father on the poverty of my vocabulary rather than on the veracity of my affirmation.

Originally, our gas masks had to be carried everywhere. The exception was to the school toilets. Visits there during class time were vigorously discouraged, a habit which naturally led to some mishaps, much to the discomfiture of the more timorous pupils. However, were one to be compelled by nature, then the gas mask could be left under your seat in class pending your prompt return. It was always confidently assumed that in the event of a gas attack by the Nazi hordes, good primary pupils would all return "in an orderly fashion" as it was put, to their desks and await further instructions. Many of us took the view that the one and only good use to which the wretched things might have been put would have been to make such visits tolerable.

The first method of carrying gas masks was to thread a piece of string under the lid just where it was "hinged" and to sling the box over the shoulder so that the lip of the lid which would be normally tucked into the box was distal to one's body. This was said to make for quick action in the event of need. The same teacher who controlled the up-tempo stair marching quickly enacted that all gas masks would be worn over the right shoulder with the box at waist level on the left side. In reality, the box and the mask was as often as not used as an assaultive weapon, as a goal post marker or as a support for one's schoolbag as for anything else.

The string, of course, constantly had to be renewed and in no time gas mask cases in oilcloth or fabric came on the scene. Initially, these were run up by clever Mums on the sewing machine but later could be bought in the shops with proper shoulder straps. In the cities it eventually came to be that one could, if so minded, buy from certain department stores commercially made gas masks which were just that bit more refined than the regular Government free issue. Needless to say, very few, if any of us out in "the sticks"availed ourselves of such luxuries.

PREPARATIONS

About this time, the local picture house had been showing the adventures of a swashbuckling Latin by the name of Zorro. There was "Zorro", "The Return of Zorro", "The Mark of Zorro" and so on. Since we could gain entry of a Saturday to these high dramas by dint of sixpence and two jam jars or lemonade bottles, the true afficionados became well versed in new styles with the sabre and epee; familiar with swinging on chandeliers; sliding down bannisters, sword "en garde"; and a tough line in bellicose and provocative taunts uttered in a pigeon lingo heavy with Franco/Spanish/Banffshire accents. In the course of the gang warfare remarked on earlier, the Sandyhillers (our gang) were running a (relatively transient) hate campaign against one boy, whose self explanatory, though not always deserved nickname, need not be mentioned. He was not minded to be one of us though living within our precinct.

Having discarded the "Jannie's" flintlocks in favour of wooden sabres, seriously sharpened and pointed to make them properly lethal, we were wont to pursue this poor lad from school to his very salubrious home nearby. We had seen in the cinema a variety of post-medieval warriors and Red Indians apparently hardening their arrow and sword points in fire. Wood and iron react rather differently to tempering by fire, as we found out, but in spite of our difficulties with the physics of the process, we were quick to follow suit and our sword points were consequently soot blackened from our efforts. One day, our feints and thrusts against the object of our disparagement became a shade vigorous and several large Z's (the mark of Zorro) were left indelibly on his gas mask case. It was our misfortune that the lad's aunt, who had brought him up, not only became aware of the "mark of Zorro", but also found that it had become virtually indelible. It was our further misfortune that the self-same auntie was a teacher at the Academy, the centre of learning to which we, because of our precocity in other matters, had just graduated from Primary school.

We were summoned to her classroom at lunchtime next day. We already guessed that it was not to be about our algebra or geometry, although, ill placed as we were to judge, it seemed that she was a good enough teacher of those subjects. This stern lady spat venom at us for a time through her tight, and, as it seemed to us, bloodless lips. She tended to use her mouth rather lopsidedly, had a naturally light voice (for a teacher!) and tended to hiss her words in a way that imbued them with added menace.

We knew, however, that her prowess with the strap was limited and we regularly took the precaution of rubbing resin from the "Fir Widdie" into our hands to harden the skin against such leathery assaults. The three of us concerned were given the option of several hundred lines each to the effect that "I must not abuse the property of other boys", or six of the strap. Zorro would have had no qualms about such a penalty. Indeed he would have bared his back to the flogger with a flourish, curled his lip in a snarl of defiance and never flinched while the torturer did his worst. We cut the dramatics (lest the Rector get wind of the episode) and took our punishment like men. We knew the story would get out and that our fame was secure for that week at least.

Regular use of the strap - the "tawse" or the "tag" as we were wont to call it - was a feature of school in those days. Even the youngest children were not exempt and all through Primary and Secondary school the swish and crack of the strap could be heard many times a day. I have never subscribed to the view that it did us good, or at worst, no harm. Many pupils had their self-esteem progressively, and often unjustifiably, eroded by repeated punishments not for inexcusable episodes of antisocial or disgusting behaviour, but for errors or omissions in academic endeavours which were, in themselves, unlikely to be of any lasting significance.

Two occasions, late in my school life in the 5th year of Secondary education, have ever since led me to wonder at the mentality of a highly educated man who could then belt me in front of the class, once for not knowing the gender of the Latin word "rus", (which I am still not sure of) and later still for twice using the subjunctive incorrectly in a mock "Higher" paper. The fact that my mark for the paper was well over 80%, top of the class, as it happened, did not absolve me since it was his view that these were careless errors that I need not have made. That, to this day, rankles. The relatively few times that I was strapped in the Primary school and lower down the Secondary for much more justified reasons have left much less resentment. Many who were routinely strapped may have warranted it at first, but even then, without the formal knowledge of psychology I have since acquired, I had cause to wonder how it could be deemed an effective way to change behaviour when it was meted out most of the time to recidivists. Intuitively, many of us recognised then that it had little to do with changing behaviour - and much more to do with the expression of power and sometimes of frustration and anger.

On the occasions like the "mark of Zorro" incident, we almost expected to be strapped. It was a simple expression of victory for the teacher (the bosses) in the unceasing war within a war we waged during these years. But there were no grudges about that. It was the way things were. We even invited punishment at times in our shameful and quite puny attempts to express some autonomy. It was the practice (on pain of - you guessed it - the strap!) for all boys to salute, by touching the forelock or tip of the cap, any teacher whether in the corridors of power in the school or on the streets of the town, during school hours or out of them. Some, indeed most, of the teachers rewarded this courtesy with a smile or a greeting which personalised the exchange and made the duty more tolerable. Some did not even look at you when you saluted and a few even criticised efforts not quite up to Sandhurst standards.

One day after school, three of us (in the Sandyhillers gang) decided we'd had enough of the offhandedness of one such teacher. We knew she was bound to pass us on the street after 4pm but decided simply to say "Good afternoon", but to keep our hands unequivocally by our sides. As usual, she failed to respond in any way till the morrow, when we were called to her classroom and "whipped" as she liked to call it. Naturally, our proposed bravado had been suitably publicised beforehand so there were pupil witnesses. No teacher required any such - her word was enough to vouch for our guilt - but we did. The open demonstration of rebellion had to be seen and the subsequent strapping (three on each hand) heard, for us to glow in the approbation of our fellow pupils. The resin came in handy again. But those were worthy skirmishes and we bore no resentment in such circumstances. We were even more likely to be picked for the football team because we had proved we were "nae safties". That seemed to be a requirement for all of us if we were to do well in the war.

It was strange how, in its earliest years, the war itself seemed to be mentioned very little in school. It may be that the Education Authority had advised teachers to "normalise" our little lives as much as possible. Apart from the blackout blinds and the tape on the windows and our ever-present gas masks, it would have been hard to tell from a casual scrutiny of our day-to-day classroom lives that anything out of the ordinary had happened.

Between September 1939 and the end of 1940, nothing changed at all in the upper Primary classes from which I was soon to be advanced. The morning rituals of Bible study, arithmetic problems "round the class" with us all standing in a circle round the walls and pupils being moved up or down the rank order depending on whether we gave the right answer or not, continued as usual. Then came my forte - "general knowledge", and geography, and these too were pursued as if the bombings, the debacle on the beaches of France, the Atlantic sinkings and the departure of most of the young men from the town were all happening on another planet. We were never excused being a bit late for school even if there had been an air raid warning lasting three hours in the middle of the previous night. In history, we still "did the Romans" of 54 and 55BC, and then "the Vikings" without any reference to the fact that the former had become our enemies again and the latter were at that very moment struggling for their lives to escape across the North Sea, not to rape and pillage but to seek a base from which to launch a later assault aimed at regaining their own country from the German oppressors.

The independence, the parochialism and, to a degree, the self-sufficiency of the Northeast mentality was preparation enough. We did not by any means ignore the war but "getting on in school" was a business with far longer precedent in our neck of the woods than was a distraction like World War 2. Quoth Miss Turner, a diminutive but fiery mentor of the upper Primary, "You boys have plenty of time to read about the war in your own time when you get home and have finished your homework. Pay attention to your lessons and the war will look after itself!" And that was just what happened.

CHAPTER 4

PRECAUTIONS

The preparation for war seemed to extend much longer than I thought it properly ought to. If this is all the rate it goes at, I thought, maybe it will last long enough for me to be a Spitfire pilot after all. At first, the press in the parlour (a tall shelved cupboard in the wall with a full sized door) was progressively emptied of ashets and cake stands, toast racks and teapots and refilled with boxes of tea and innumerable tin cans of beans, bully beef, steamed puddings (would you believe?), tinned pears and other goodies. My mother had a thing about tea. She had always bought it from an Edinburgh wholesaler who in turn imported it direct from Ceylon. It came, every six months or so, in a foil lined plywood teabox about two and a half feet cubed. My interest was always more in the box - for the gang hut, as a potential table, chair or store cupboard - than in the tea. However, when the war broke out, the box was retained in the press together with the tea. It was retained against unspoken exigencies. A year later, it was emptied by innumerable servicemen and women who came for meals while billeted locally or in transit. No more tea arrived.

One of the byproducts of my experience of the press and its contents during the war, together with the need (of which we were constantly reminded by parents, press and teachers) to be ready for all sorts of emergencies, was that I myself, even as an adult, and long past the war, still tend to hoard. When shopping, I will tend, now in a land of plenty, to buy two or three items, especially of tinned foods and things like biscuits, when one would do. My sense of a siege economy has never quite left me and unconsciously I must have been greatly influenced by my mother's anticipation of later hardships by the press's contents.

Other purchases necessitated by the times were yards and yards of blackout cloth and yards and yards of tape or old lace or cheese cloth curtains. Because we lived in an old Scottish manse with huge, tall windows and many rooms, the problems of light proofing were great - and costly. For a time, a parish minister's salary being much less than princely, several rooms had no blackout provision at all and as a result, no lights were usable after dark. In a North Scottish winter, that was for a long time. Gradually, however, my mother ran up on the old treadle sewing machine enough black cotton blinds to cover all the windows. In retrospect, such was the quality of the gaslight and paraffin lamps we used in the house that I doubt if any but the most eagle-eyed of Nazi pilots would have seen anything at all from more than 500 feet up.

The Air Raid Wardens were, however, in the absence of any real action involving either "blood, sweat, toil or tears", frighteningly assiduous in their duties to ensure that no Banff or Macduff fifth columnist (as spies or traitors were then known) spent his evenings flashing secret torch messages to U-boats in the bay. Should a draught, of which there were many, happen to flip a curtain half an inch from the edge of the window sash, a couple of fierce blasts on his whistle and, "Put out that light!", would immediately ring from the street. Wardens had this odd quality of being at the same time ubiquitous, officious and efficient. Government policy had dictated that ARP personnel would be a volunteer cadre which, in England especially, was drawn almost exclusively from the middle classes. The workers' reticence to assume even the slight authority provided by an official armband and whistle excluded them from such a force and this was to result, certainly in the early months of the war, in the Wardens being seen, probably somewhat unfairly, as a rather jumped-up band of interferers. Angus Calder, Constantine Fitzgibbon and Norman Longmate, in their documentary volumes about life in Britain during the early years of the war in particular, all remark on this curious social phenomenon. My memories are that the very awareness of class in Scotland was, and always has been, much less marked than it was south of the border and that there was a much broader social spectrum represented among the Wardens. Nevertheless they did certainly share in the peremptory style attributed to them - and were perhaps even a bit proud of it. Of course, when in the course of the heavy bombings of London and the other main cities of both Scotland, Wales and England, they showed themselves to be as brave, assiduous and resourceful as any in the war, the balance of attitudes toward them turned remarkably.

One war historian, T H O'Brien, described the blackout as having "transformed conditions of life more thoroughly than any other single feature of the war". Quite apart from the amount of money which all householders had to find to pay for blackout materials, there was the time it took every evening ensuring that each and every chink at a window or door, skylight or lobby was thoroughly covered against the escape of light. Cars, buses and trains ran with little or no light showing and it came as no surprise when Government statistics for late 1939 and early 1940 showed that the total number of people killed in road accidents had increased by 100%. These figures excluded all the incidental and accidental happenings whereby poor benighted (literally) souls were killed or injured by falling off railway platforms, stepping into rivers and ponds, falling through glass roofs or walking into hidden obstructions on the street. At that time, newspaper reports suggested that about one person in five was likely to have suffered injury, fortunately not all serious, due to some accident caused by the blackout.

There were, of course, no street lights whatsoever. While this mattered little during the long summer nights, it did pose some problems during the winter. We all acquired small torches not only to find our way home but also, more importantly, to mark our presence to the occasional bus or car, usually military, struggling to keep to the road with its own lights limited to three inch slits about a quarter of an inch deep in the black metal plates fastened over the headlights. These torches were a godsend to small boys who liked to read in bed. Given that much of that reading was from comics such as the "Wizard", "Hotspur"or the "Beano", or for us "intellectuals", "Dixon Hawke and Tommy Burke, his Boy Assistant", they did allow of instant dowsing the moment a parental step was heard on the landing, and they had to be in the bedroom lest the siren should signal yet another determined German raid on Banff and we had to find our way down to the shelter in pitch darkness.

It is easy to forget that the other aspect of the blackout, with all the blinds, thick curtains and black cloth over the windows, is that, after lights out, the interior of houses were in Stygian darkness.

Then, there was no question of simply pressing a switch. Matches had to be found, a candle or oil lamp lit, or the gas turned on and carefully lit without breaking the desperately fragile mantle(s) which were themselves in short supply. With a late twentieth century awareness of Health and Safety at Work and in the Home, I shudder to think now of how I habitually read in bed under a canopy of bedclothes held up by my knees while a candle on a tin lid burned alongside the book in this cosy little tent. The torches at least did away with all that! Naturally, such activities were forbidden by my parents, as was some of my reading matter, but one had to be a bit surreptitious because the light shone under the door if the candle was at the bedside.

There was one interesting evening when my father came home sporting a cracker of a black eye and a deep and dramatic cut across his nose and forehead. Mother's obvious solicitude ruled her out as the assailant and I doubted whether any of the Women's Guild packed that kind of a punch with a rolled umbrella or well swung handbag. In any case, father was much too genial a man with the townsfolk for any easy explanation of his injury to spring to mind. It transpired that he had left a meeting in the Church Hall in High Street, crossed the road without having had benefit of torchlight. He had the confidence of long familiarity and promptly and without warning walked straight into a cast iron lamp post on the other side of the street, knocking himself out and having to recover with the help of passers by in the doorway of the adjacent shop. He had just become one of the "one in five's" to suffer injury in the blackout. From then on my brother and I were schooled by him on how explore pitch darkness by moving forward with both hands outstretched, fingers of each hand entwined with those of the other, so that there would be no chance of repeating his error of feeling ahead of him with hands apart. They had passed easily on each side of the lamp post.

So much for the blackout! The tape and lace curtains were more easily dealt with. We all spent a merry afternoon or two mixing batter paste and smearing it over the windows before stretching lengths of tape crisscross over the glass. The old lace curtains were pasted over the windows at the rear of the house, where the loss of light was not going to affect father's work. The purpose of all this was of course to prevent flying slivers of glass in the event of bomb blast. Little did we think that one day not too far distant, it would serve that very purpose.

The final excitement of those months was the preparation of the "black hole", not of Calcutta, but of the Manse. It was to be our air raid shelter because it was deemed that our substantial stone house of three storeys, at the core of which was this little den under the staircase, would withstand bombs and/or shellfire better than an Anderson shelter. For some people, especially in the cities, the Anderson shelter (named after the then Home Secretary) was the preferred safety resource in the event of bombing. This was a smallish - about six feet by five feet - structure with a curved roof of corrugated steel which was half buried in the garden, reinforced with sandbags and heaped earth and usually containing minimal amenities, rudimentary survival rations and water and a candle for light if needed. With a small earth-reinforced steel blast wall built up in front of the entrance, an Anderson shelter would withstand almost anything other than a direct hit. Up to six persons could shelter in one and my oldest aunt and her family had regular recourse to theirs in south London over a period of several of the war years, especially in 1940 and 1941.

Tragically, one of my cousins, a sailor who had survived many convoys in the Atlantic, came home on leave during a bombing raid on London, stayed safe in the Anderson shelter in the garden until the "All Clear" siren sounded. The rest of the family remained in the shelter for a little longer while he went into the damaged house (Aunt Mary was bombed out four times in all) to make them a cup of tea. Two minutes later, before the kettle had boiled, he was blown to bits by a huge explosion. A delayed action bomb had hit the house earlier without its having been noticed amid the general cacophony of the raid and had only then blown up.

The shelters themselves were considered to be a good bargain. They cost between £6 and £10 and were sold to anyone earning over £250 per year. Those earning less got them free. One snag was that they were just a bit too short to allow a bed to fit in and many were found to flood much too readily after rain or when dug in in low-lying ground. In fact, the shortage of steel which ensued by early 1940 led to the supply being discontinued and the government then engaged in a policy of building surface shelters of brick and concrete for much larger numbers of people. These were what we finally had in the school backyards. We, as schoolboys, enjoyed them for reasons other than safety but Angus Calder, in "The People's War" did not enthuse about them.

> "These squat erections were the common type of shelter in many working class districts. Their ventilation was limited; they were cold, dark and damp; even where chemical closets were provided, they stank and sometimes overflowed.Not surprisingly, the surface shelters were generally unpopular, especially when they showed a disconcerting tendency to collapse, through poor construction, when bombs fell near by."

Most folks were content simply to find some relatively strong and secure part of their home which could be converted into an air raid shelter. The government suggested that the area under the stairs was usually the strongest part of the house and great ingenuity was exercised by thousands of families as to how they could strengthen and enhance in a variety of ways such a shelter. There were times furth of our area when families spent most nights, or part of most nights, in the shelter, listening, after the wail of the air raid warning siren, for the ominous throb characteristic of the BMW radial engines of the German bombers. The resonant beat as the twin engines fell in and out of phase immediately proclaimed them as "one of theirs!" The deep thud of exploding bombs and the rattle of machine gun fire confirmed it.

The Manse was a substantially built house, pretentious in the style of the late 19th century, cold as charity, but built to stand for hundreds of years. The cupboard under the stairs referred to earlier was the unlit, slightly musty, area where the maid, or, less often, my mother, found the sweeper, the carpet beaters, the garden broom, preserving jars, a three year old bunch of onions long since forgotten and now sporting a beard and rich in penicillin, and to me, inexplicably, a large terracotta tub of eggs in a preservative called eisenglas. The latter seemed wholly disgusting to me and I shuddered to watch anyone reach into the glutinous mess to extricate an egg from time to time. For some reason, no alternative resting place could be found for this vessel, which had the odd property of never emptying no matter how many eggs were used. This simply added to its ghostly, even fiendish qualities.

Thus it was that, as the Heinkel 111's and Junkers 88's dived on and strafed the patrol boats in the bay, I would curl up in the bunk we shared in the

The Manse, Banff, photographed in 1939

"black hole" secretly stressed by the fantasy, not of the whole house tumbling about my ears from a direct hit, but by the prospect of that unwholesome mess of eggs and gunge being spattered over all and sundry. I had not at that time been made aware of any other "fate worse than death".

There was always a certain ambivalence about having recourse to the "black hole". On the one hand, it offered all the romance of candle or oil lamp light, one of the features which could just about hint at cosiness in that cramped and musty pit. There was a legitimate excuse to read late at night and there was just a sufficient frisson of excitement and perhaps a tincture of fear to stir the blood.

On the other hand, my father had the annoying habit of rising every few minutes, it seemed, to visit the back door to see if there was anything significant going on - gazing skywards in the pitch darkness - the fourth wise man, I thought, anticipating another star in the east perhaps. Mind you, with him in his pyjamas and woolly checked dressing gown and bereft of his dog-collar, he somehow lacked the necessary authority to call down signs and portents from the heavens. The trouble was that he let the most bone chilling of draughts sweep through the house every time he did it. The candle wavered, my goose pimples quivered individually and wafts of the dreaded eisenglas assailed my nostrils. My mother would get anxious about those forays.

"Daddy, come in and shut that door! You can't see anything

out there!" She was always strong on telling people what they could and couldn't see and what they thought or ought to think. Meanwhile, my brother, not much given to reading then, and as phlegmatic as he has remained to this day, slept peacefully in his little bunk against the wall.

Early in the war, the threat of air attack was taken quite seriously throughout the country, and with the egocentricity of hardened parochialism, the small towns took this threat to heart as much as the cities. Partly this was because as a seaside town, ours was seen to offer possible invasion beaches to the enemy and partly because many small towns in remoter areas were also seen as useful places to smuggle away a variety of military units, some regrouping and re-equipping after a failed raid on the enemy and some training and planning clandestine operations for the future. Any reasonably fit (i.e. warm and vertical) males left in the town after the call-up of the others tended to be in the LDV force - Local Defence Volunteers, or, as they came to be known then, the "Look, Duck and Vanish" boys, and later, "Dad's Army" or the Home Guard.

If they were not, then joining the Royal Observer Corps was an option. The latter frequented two kinds of habitat. The first of these were little round sandbagged emplacements on the tops of hills or on high buildings. They contained little more than a telephone, a set of reasonably high-powered binoculars and a pelorus, a simple device to assess the azimuth and elevation of any aircraft spotted. If they happened to be recognised as hostile, the type, number and direction of the raiders would then be reported by telephone to the Fighter Command Sector HQ for appropriate action. The second of the ROC's habitats were local drill or church halls the walls of which were hung not with medieval tapestries but with large and varied silhouette plan and elevation drawings (all carefully to scale) of every known type of British, American, German, Italian and later, Japanese aircraft likely to be used in the war.

There were also, published by Penguin Books, a series of aircraft recognition volumes which every boy worth his salt would possess, which recapitulated these drawings together with all known performance data about these aircraft. These were seldom out of our pockets. If teachers could have seen the assiduousness with which we devoured those books and quizzed each other on our detailed knowledge, they would have wondered at our apparent reluctance to acquire other kinds of knowledge during the school day. Of course, there were also volumes of British aircraft, the more likely to be spotted ones being already well known to us. At that time, the Vickers Supermarine "Spitfire" was naturally recognised by all the lads as the most superb, and beautiful, flying machine. In fact, the sight of any aircraft flying overhead in the north of Scotland during the years prior to the war was enough to bring not only us boys but also some adults to their back doors to gaze in admiration and wonder. After all, the Wright brothers had cracked the secret of heavier than air flight only just over thirty years before.

Occasionally a biplane such as a Gloster "Gladiator" or Captain Fresson's De Havilland "Rapide" on the Aberdeen to Orkney run would come within eyeball range over Banff. From September 1939, however, air traffic over the North became more frequent as military airfields at Dyce, Lossiemouth, Crimond and Kinloss became operational. "Whitley" bombers, twin engined and twin ruddered, but not so slim in profile as the German Dornier 217's would drone past at relatively low levels. On occasion we would also see a "Wellington" with its revolutionary geodetic airframe design, and, most thrilling of all, a "Hurricane" or "Spitfire" would swoop low over the coast. Then we certainly would rush to look and admire. In school, scant attention was paid to the teacher until it was distressingly clear that the passing aircraft was not going to be visible from the windows of the classroom we were then inhabiting. If it were to be seen from our benches, then a natural break occurred in the flow of the lesson.

At that stage of the war, few serious attacks were being made over the Scottish mainland and although the wailing of the siren would wake us from sleep from time to time in the night or send some of us scampering for home during the day, the few German aircraft to intrude limited themselves to a bomb and machine gun attack on the armed trawlers which patrolled the bays along the coast against the intrusion of minelaying or secret agent-bearing U-boats.

Very early in the war there was a flurry of activity along the shore-line of Banff and Macduff, and indeed on every beach and bay around the British coastline. The German war machine was seen to pose threats from both sea and sky and such had been the initial success of the Blitzkrieg in Europe that invasion by paratroopers and glider-borne Wehrmacht or by landing craft on the sandy beaches was immediately anticipated.

Lorry loads of Royal Engineers, Pioneer Corps and other miscellaneous workers materialised on the beaches at Banff links, the Palmer cove and at the mouth of the Deveron. Within hours, rolls of barbed wire were staked with iron posts into the ground at a height of 4 or 5 feet all the way from the west side of Whitehills to the east end of Banff Bridge. There were no breaks in this particular defence and we knew instinctively that our happy days playing on the sand, in the sea, and making rafts on the "Bandies", as an inlet of the river Deveron just above the bridge was called, had ended. No more digging of major canals in the sand, no more searching for nests by the river bank and no more football on the fine flat bit of grass along the shore between the bridge and the "Stinkin' Lochie". And if we were concerned about "our" wee bit of the coast, it was no more than was happening all around the shores of Britain.

For in no time at all the whole area of the sand from the high to low tide marks was spiked with firmly anchored poles about twelve feet tall spaced at regular intervals of perhaps 50 feet from each other. They would be there, some skewed by storm and sea, and but for a few gone for ever in some gale, for another six years or so. These were the more obvious hazards. The intention was that they would deter the landing of troop carrying gliders on the sand at low tide. Other more secret deterrents were also being planted in the form of land mines all along the links and on every bit of grassy shore that might allow access to our land.

We watched, after school, the Engineers cut out the turf and "plant" the flat canisters in the shallow holes in the sandy soil, carefully fit the fuse and move on to the next a few yards away. Once the turf had been replaced, with great care, even delicacy, there was little within a day or two to indicate the lethal charges underlying it. Large signs in red exclaiming "Danger! Mines!" warned us of the hazards but several adventurous non-readers among the local dogs met a premature demise if they were big and heavy enough.

PRECAUTIONS

There also arose among the more delinquent of us an almost irresistible impulse to trigger a satisfying explosion by throwing large stones into the minefields in the hope that one might land on a mine. The danger of being injured by flying shrapnel seemed less than being nicked by the Bobby or being waylaid by some members of one of the hostile gangs we tended to develop internecine wars with. After some years, all the minefields became pitted with small craters where boys or dogs had set off mines and the rest of the areas accumulated a collection of stones of varying sizes - a few deposited by winter storms, but many the result of these juvenile experiments.

There were nice distinctions to be made between choosing stones that were heavy enough to set off a mine but not so heavy as to be too heavy to cast far enough for the thrower to be safe from blast and shrapnel and those that could be heaved from a safe distance but were still big enough to do the job. A few of us thought that each mine so triggered meant one more German might penetrate the defences of the United Kingdom, but most simply saw the exercise as another boyish ploy. There was always a great bang with sand and stones flying and a residual pall of black smoke - seldom fully appreciated since the miscreant would hot-foot it into the distance as soon as the stone was flung. A few would watch nonchalantly from their bikes till the police or ARP Warden arrived, ready to claim that they too had heard the bang and had just that moment arrived!

However, once in a while tragedy would strike. Around the coast cases came to light of children crawling through the barbed wire to get a ball or such like and finishing up maimed or dead. One Saturday morning, I think, for I was not at school, there was yet another explosion from the shore and the familiar column of black smoke. That was the one which finished my interest in the minefields for ever and left me to grieve for a lost friend.

Some four or five years before, I was not quite succeeding in coping with my first day at Primary school. A toughie from a higher class had grabbed my school cap, new navy blue serge with the BXA badge embroidered on the front, and flung it up on to the flat, rain soaked roof of the boys' lavatories. Devoid of the necessary social or pugilistic skills to remedy the situation, I was near to tears when a wee lad, more worldly wise and vigorous than myself came up.

"Nivver mind, Davie. Ah'll get yir cap an' gie 'im a beltin'."

I snivelled my thanks as Sanders (as he was known) shinned up the soil pipe on to the roof, flung down my bonnet, climbed down with great expertise and pursued my assaulter before giving him a satisfactory thumping. No teacher appeared. Sanders was that sort of boy. He was popular, helpful, bright and cheerful. What was his academic status we neither knew nor cared. But he was always welcome on your side in the playground football and I became friendly with him from that day on. He was always ready to help. On that awful Saturday morning he may well have been behaving true to form and perhaps had tried to rescue from behind the barbed wire a ball or toy for someone else. He died in the task. How often have I thought of his cheerful, puckish face since. He must in his short life have filled more people's lives with happy memories than mine.

The final stages of the coastal defence system took longer. There were huge (about 6 foot cubed) concrete blocks placed as tank barriers at points on the beaches where tracked vehicles might attempt to breach the mine and wire defences. Indeed after the war these were amongst the last evidences of conflict to be removed - and a difficult task it was! Several appeared along the Palmer cove and by the Boyndie burn and concrete blockhouses were built at strategic points such as near the end of the bridge. Several of these have remained around the countryside of what was then Banffshire to this day, a few, such as one on the end of Banff harbour east pier finishing up as (unofficial) none too salubrious public lavatories. All this, the blackout, the air raid siren going off from time to time and the daily list of casualties in the paper left us in no doubt that our futures were far from secure.

In 1940 and 1941 there were actually more minor raids than one might nowadays have expected on these small Northern communities. Several of them were simply aborted missions, breakaways from more major targets, in the course of which the German aircrew, anxious to return home without their bombload and to declare to their Nazi masters their dutifully hostile intentions by empty machine gun magazines, jettisoned everything they could. Nevertheless, there were some casualties and considerable damage in the towns and villages of Banffshire, Moray and Aberdeenshire and more than a few in the city of Aberdeen.

These raids were, however, symptomatic of the great number of air assaults being made at that time to much more damaging effect on the cities of England and London in particular. My parents tried several times - in vain - to persuade my aunt Mary and cousin Millie to leave London and to come up north where it was apparently safer. They, true Londoners in everything but birth, preferred to remain where they were in spite of everything. Millie was working in a munitions factory and my uncle worked on the railways down there so they hung on till the war ended. My uncle and cousin died and the family lost all their worldly goods on three occasions due to the bombing but they never tired of telling how, after one particularly severe air raid, their house in Croydon had completely disintegrated leaving only a huge smoking crater at the foot of which lay their Marconi wireless set. They rescued it, wiped it down, turned it on and, lo and behold, - it played perfectly! Always with an eye to an opportunity, aunt Mary wrote up the story of the wireless and sent it in to the Marconi factory. A brand new set was immediately sent to the family for the use of the story for advertising purposes.

After the issue of gas masks, the next administrative move from the authorities (so far as we schoolchildren were concerned) was for our teachers to establish whether we could, within, I think it was, five minutes of the air raid warning being sounded, run home from school. Were it to take longer than that, then we were to be herded into the shelters at the school just described - spartan, hastily constructed, unlit brick and concrete roofed structures with wooden benches, near the playground. Those unlucky enough to have homes within about half a mile of the school were thus excluded - to their chagrin - from all the dukery-packery with the girls that was foreseen by the more lascivious spirits to be opportune in these damp and darkened chambers.

It was only on researching in the press archives for a recent public lecture about some aspects of the early war years that I discovered that the whole business of our trying to get home in five minutes had been instigated by my father who was then a member of the local School Management Committee. A joint meeting of that body with the Banff Town Council was reported in the "Banffshire Journal" of 11 June 1940 when there was apparently some vigorous discussion and debate about the pros and cons of such a plan as proposed by Rev Findlay Clark. The Rector of the Academy, for reasons not reported, had opposed the proposal but a vote led to my father's motion prevailing. Father's arguments had apparently been that by letting as many children home as possible there was dispersion of risk in the event of the school receiving a direct hit and there would also be some reduction of anxiety on the part of parents who would prefer to have their children at home with them during a raid.

We were also given rather impromptu lessons by our teachers, in collaboration with the Air raid Wardens, on how to smother incendiary bombs with buckets of sand or with a stirrup pump. The latter was so called because it consisted of a simple cylinder pump with about an 18 inch stroke, held vertical into a bucket of water by the "stirrup", a metal leg fixed to the top of the cylinder but offset by a few inches to allow it to run outside the bucket parallel to the cylinder down to the ground where it terminated in a stirrup-like foot plate which held it steady while one pulled and pumped vertically with the handle and plunger. With not inconsiderable effort a rather puny stream could be directed four or five yards on to "the source of the fire" (as the bomb was always described). A push button control at the nozzle of the hose attached to the pump allowed either a spray or a jet of water to be used as necessary. Gardeners found these very useful.

Consequently the stirrup pumps supplied at intervals along the corridors of schools were all counted regularly by the Janitor and the Warden. The sand buckets sitting, with at least one water bucket, alongside the pumps became the insalubrious receptacles of (presumably) the teachers' fag ends. The pupils' were ground under foot in the playground or flushed away in the lavatories. The dog ends in the fire buckets were most likely to have been planted after school hours when certain teachers and a few lucky senior pupils were acting as Fire Watchers on a roster every night of the week. Stories of what went on as they scanned the night sky for falling incendiaries or paraded the upstairs corridors and attics were legion

- but quite unrepeatable in the light of the libel laws.

Very early in the war a Public Information Leaflet (of which there were to be many) was issued to every household. This stated, in heavy type, **"If you throw a bucket of water on a burning incendiary bomb, it will explode and throw burning fragments in all directions"**. The further instructions on the paper described how such bombs should be smothered in sand or with a sandbag. In spite of the apparent clarity of such an instruction it was reported late in 1939 by Mass Observation that only 33% of Londoners interviewed on the subject could give a correct answer as to what should be done. Constantine Fitz Gibbon, in his book on "The Blitz", quotes some of the quainter notions of these interviewees about what should be done, along with the commonest response. The latter was, "Throw the bomb into water" or "Throw water over the bomb". Among the others were: "Stand up by a brick wall", "Lay on it" (sic), "Leave it to a Warden", "Flop a coat over it, or throw it into a sewer, or anywhere there is water", "Pick it up and run it in water", "Sit back and hold tight"; more sensibly, "Leave it where it was and run", and, more bizarrely, "Keep the thin places of your house patched up" and "Put on your gas mask".

In the light of that it was little wonder that a continuous campaign of public education about fire fighting the incendiaries was instituted. Apart from our practice in the schools with sand buckets and stirrup pumps, there were advertised public demonstrations at times when people of all ages would not be at work. The faithful "Banffshire Journal" of one week in May 1940 reported that Banff Picture House would be showing "Jamaica Inn" with Charles Laughton as the star and, on the same bill, for we got two "pictures" as we called them at each "house", Errol Flynn and Olivia de Havilland in "The Adventures of Robin Hood". I remember going to see them quite well, in flickery black and white, the pictures that is, not me. It cost me 9d.

In that week, however, it was not by any means the only entertainment in the town. The "Banffie" as it is called to this day, simultaneously carried a report of an event which carried an unmistakable overtone of farce to lighten the gloom of our national situation. There was to be a practical demonstration to the lieges on how to deal properly with incendiary bombs run by Sergeant Strachan of the local police and a Mr F Ritchie, the local ARP Equipment Officer. They had carefully set up a false corrugated iron roof on top of four posts over a pail of water. The intention was to display how quickly the magnesium based flames of the incendiary bomb they had obtained for the demonstration would burn right through the metal "roof", and would then fall into the pail of water.

Unfortunately, after a suitably sombre preamble to the firewatchers and other members of the public present, the specimen bomb, having been ignited, promptly and with much fizzing and intense flame, burned through the corrugated iron - but completely missed the pail of water and rolled away down the slight slope of the site towards the watchers. Not surprisingly, this caused a brisk scattering of the previously attentive crowd, and Messrs Strachan and Ritchie! It was later explained that had the bomb fallen into the pail of water as intended, then it would have been obvious that the water would not have doused it and it would have promptly burned through the water-filled pail bottom as well. We should therefore use sand to stifle such a fire as every right-minded citizen had, by the press and Leaflets, already been well instructed.

The following week's "Banffie" was glad to report a repeat performance of the demonstration by the same personnel at Buckie which apparently went a bit better and the bomb hit the bucket as planned.

The unremitting cultural awareness of the "Banffie" of these days was such that, alongside of such action-packed reporting, there was a lengthy report of the celebration of the centenary of the death of the author Thomas Hardy in Dorchester (the Casterbridge of the novels) where Lord Baldwin gave appropriate speeches. Maintaining the almost surreal juxtaposition of events reported at that time, within a period of but a week or two, there were reports in the paper of Italy declaring war on the Allies (the other side was known as the Axis) and of the capitulation of France. The story of German troops riding in triumph through Paris was jammed between reports on how St Mary's Church Hall was to become a Depot for the collection and cleaning of sphagnum moss and of the excellent social evening run by Monquihitter WRI.

CHAPTER 5

EVACUATION

At about this time, and after a rather gloomy session of re-adjusting the Swastikas and Union Jacks on my map on the parlour wall as the Panzer Divisions closed around Dunkirk, father called a family conference. Such portentous meetings almost never occurred in our family. Indeed, finding all four of us in the house at any one time was quite unusual such was the fractured timetabling of events, including meals, in a Manse. We knew it was portentous by the fact that mother also came in looking serious. The cat and the maid were both excluded from the proceedings. After a brief resume of the war so far and an explanation of the pros and the cons of the evacuation of children, we were told that there was an opportunity for Tom, my brother, and myself to be evacuated to Canada for the duration of the war.

We would be shipped from the Clyde within a fortnight and billeted with a family in some unspecified part of Canada. There was no question of our parents accompanying us but the choice was ours - isolated safety (provided we survived the Atlantic crossing) against the risk of occasional bombs or a Nazi invasion and all that that might involve. From the vantage point of contemporary history it is easy to think that a decision to stay put in Scotland would have taken little or no time to make. Then, however, there was the knowledge of a series of swingeing defeats for our forces in Europe, the consequent stories of hardship, imprisonment of the innocent and the torture and sometimes murder of other resisters now beginning to percolate through from sources in the defeated nations, and the real threat, keenly felt by us all, of imminent Nazi invasion somewhere on our shores.

It is hard at this distance in time to analyse quite how the eventual decision was reached. My brother, then barely eight, looked at me expectantly to see whether a land of lumberjacks, cowboys and Indians held sufficient enchantment for us to engage in this unexpected adventure. We had seen enough of Hopalong Cassidy and the 'Cisco Kid to know the language but the Movietone News items about the sinking of the "Athenia" and the hazards of the convoys were less than encouraging. We could not be sure either whether the Canadians had Dinky toys, chip shops and "Green Finals" telling us about Deveronvale and Clachnacuddin on a Saturday night - and anyway, our parents, we supposed, weren't too bad - when they were in a good mood. So I said we'd stay in Scotland and chance it. Ironically, such are the twists of fate that brother Tom has now been a Canadian citizen for several decades, but that's another story. Within a week, we were to act as hosts to a squad of evacuees from Clydeside, planted by the authorities in the Manse since it was a fine big house with the space to bed them all although there was but one bath and that came in for very heavy use indeed!

That came about largely as a result of the extremely rapid passage through Parliament in May 1940 of the Emergency Powers (Defence) Act. This had the effect of virtually putting the life and property of every citizen at the beck and call of the Government at one fell swoop. Among other things, it meant that the Manse, our home, being a large and commodious house, was commandeered early for the purposes of evacuation of both civilian children and of troops. Acts of Parliament were being rushed through the House at a rate unseemly to the point of madness at about this time. A National coalition government was simply acting for the security of the state with every means at its disposal, but such precipitate legislation has never been seen since. Another such Act, the Treachery Act, in the same month, led to Fascist activists such as Sir Oswald Moseley being interned under Section 18B of the Act. Our wholehearted approval of that particular arrest was, however, much tempered by the fact that old Joe Camelli, the jolly and bluff character of an ice cream man in Low Street, was also whisked away for internment. He had always met our remorseless parodying of his rich Italianate English with mock rage and indignation, but he had really become one of us. Crowding into his shop, we would ask in "Comic Cuts" Italian for an "ice-a-da creema", to which he would reply, asking us, "You boys wanna-da-joos?" There simply seemed no probability at all that old Joe, or any of his family, were likely to set up an illicit wireless set, harbour Axis spies or signal in the night to German raiders that Banff was a likely target for their bombs. He might just have welcomed an opportunity to call in a couple of Gestapo Dobermann Pinschers to sort out our cheeky habits in his shop, and in that he might well have been fully justified. Anything more serious, however, was just not credible from what we knew of him. In the event of his internment we were much disconcerted for his family.

In Banff, as in many other small boroughs the length and breadth of the land during 1939 and '40, the Town Council was much relieved when the Rector of the Academy volunteered his teaching staff as Billeting Officers for evacuees. They were assisted in the task by ladies of the Guilds. Most evacuees to the town of Banff were thus placed in homes rather than the "hostels" which held some. The latter were no more than disused halls or old schools and they were usually intended for unusual groupings of children such as the handicapped or the disturbed.

Locally the organisation of placements was relatively well managed. It was not so in other areas. One description of the time described how in one area, the local householders simply assembled on the railway platforms as evacuees arrived off the trains and scrambled to pick "the best ones". "Scenes reminiscent of a cross between an early Roman slave market and Selfridge's bargain basement ensued". As Angus Calder put it, "Potato farmers selected husky lads; girls of ten or twelve who could lend a hand in the house were naturally much in demand; nicely dressed children were whisked away by local bigwigs. Those who got "second pick" were often resentful, and there was likely to be a residue of unwholesome looking waifs whom nobody wanted, but whom somebody would have to take when the Billeting Officer began to mutter about compulsory powers."

A rich vein of stories about serious social mismatches and the gross ignorance of some sections of the community about how the others lived can be found in several of the histories of the time. Children were given toothbrushes and had no idea what they were. Some were ticked off for urinating on the carpet, so went into the corner and did it there. City children could not cope with the deep darkness and silence of the country night and lived in terror of "ghosties" and the like. They had only ever slept to the cacophony of trams, the pubs coming out and stairhead brawls. With the heartless cruelty of many young children, the locals were quick to spot these Achilles heels and to exacerbate, both by word and deed, the incomers' difficulties. Brothers and sisters were separated from each other and the Roman Catholic children of Irish immigrant Liverpudlians were placed with deeply Calvinistic sheep farmers in the depths of Welsh speaking Wales. For most of those who came to Banff, however, such dramatic mismatches were a minority. Perhaps because it was thought that the Manse, of all places, might be the home of greater charity and understanding, we did seem to have received rather a high proportion of the mismatches.

During the early months of the war it is estimated that nearly 3.5 million people moved home from places deemed to be dangerous to those sought safer. Civil servants and businesses had begun to move from the metropolitan areas early in the war, some under the Government's "Plan Yellow" and some voluntarily. So far as parents and children were concerned, the country was divided into "evacuation", "neutral" and "reception" areas with populations of thirteen, fourteen and eighteen million people respectively. The first of these were the population centres where air raids could be expected. The second "neutral" areas would neither take nor send evacuees and the third "reception" areas, within which Banff was placed, were to take children and mothers of small children from the threatened areas. In the event, many more areas than were originally categorised in the first group were bombed, some quite heavily. Children from the vulnerable areas were shepherded by schoolteachers and volunteers onto trains and buses with the varying skill described above and despatched sometimes the length and breadth of the land to homes almost randomly selected. If, locally, there were few serious social mismatches, nationally there were many. Interestingly though, only about half the number of evacuees predicted by government at the beginning of the war actually took up the chance to become such.

The people giving billets were paid ten shillings and sixpence (about 52p in 1997) for the first child and eight shillings and sixpence per child if (s)he took more than one. This was supposed to cover full board and lodging. This flat rate might, as Angus Calder in "The People's War" pointed out, have been all right for a child billeted with an agricultural labourer, who might bring home no more than about thirty-five shillings a week, but for the middle classes, accustomed to a slightly higher standard of living, it was derisory. He pointed out too that the flat rate bore hardly on those households billeting fast-growing teenagers with ravenous appetites. Because the well-to-do tended to make their own arrangements for evacuation anyway, the bulk of evacuees being placed by local authority billeting officers in the reception areas were from deprived urban families, often with social, educational and behavioural deficits of varying severity.

When evacuees arrived at their destination - and that was often a fluke of circumstance determined by which train happened to be available at the time they gathered at the station in their home town - their disposal to homes or hostels was in the hands of one or more of these Billeting Officers. Usually the latter, as in Banff, would be local government officers of some sort but were often, especially in rural areas, volunteers from schoolteaching staffs, local Women's Guilds, the WRI and church groups. As Angus Calder remarked, "Such people naturally varied enormously in status, competence, integrity and compassion. It fell upon them to organise a social experiment of unprecedented size and difficulty."

My abiding memory of the day we received our evacuees, initially six, though two were moved elsewhere within a couple of days, was of the bath being run continually, the boiler in the kitchen having to be stoked equally continuously, with wood, coal and dross at a frightening rate to keep up the supply of hot water and my mother rushing, shocked, to the chemist's for some potion to rid the children's hair of lice and nits. They also had fleas, though they might have picked them up in the train, and I remember especially one girl whose name now eludes me, who showed me how to catch them and put them in a matchbox for later "demonstration" at school.

Some arrived in ragged clothes, all with one small case or bag and a large label tied into a buttonhole with their names and home addresses. One or two were so shocked and inarticulate that we could make little of them and since they more or less took over the house and our few toys we probably bore them a measure of resentment, at least at first. Behind the Manse was a large garden with two lawns - a drying green and a croquet lawn. The evacuees could not believe that it was not really a public park, that we actually could play football on the larger of the two areas of grass any time we liked and that vegetables really grew before their very eyes. They had never seen a garden in the back streets of where they had come from.

As my mother and the maid tore about the house in a fine frenzy of sorting clothes, learning names, bedmaking and food preparation during these hectic first few days of the influx, it became apparent that the account was not all on the debit side, however. Granted, we scratched a lot more and ate a bit less (some had come without their ration books), but on the credit side we learned a lot more swear words, picked up the rudiments of sexual experimentation, especially from one rather precocious and good looking young girl who, needless to say, my mother was none too keen on, and also learned to stand up a bit more vigorously and muscularly for ourselves. Our football also improved since there were two "tanner ba'" specialists among the Glaswegians.

Unfortunately, the whole evacuation programme nationally rapidly became a bit of a fiasco. Parents separated from their children wearied to have them back and so long as there was no immediate danger from bombing, they tended to visit once and take them back on the second or third visit. Gradually our tough little charges trickled back to their origins and a year later we were once more *in statu quo*. There were some who, for a variety of reasons, stayed on and became true adoptive citizens of their reception area. They saw out school and later, College or apprenticeship, and in time raised their own families in these northern climes. Some also brought life and pleasure to childless or jaded people and found homes that gave them opportunity and love.

The majority found their way back to the pens and the closies, the jangling stridency of the shipyards and the endless harsh battle against urban adversity. But they had seen cattle suckling their calves and the herring, silver from the sea. They had heard the morning chorus from the woodside as the birds greeted the dawn, the wind in the trees and the broad doric accents of the ploughmen. They had learned to say "Sir" to the Rector and to know the bobby by his first name - and perhaps they began to appreciate, just a little, their own parents.

There were a few who never returned to their urban origins. One of those, Robin, sat reminiscing about these days with me one evening not so long ago just as might one of my indigenous friends have done, so deeply entrenched is he in the local culture. He himself remembers having arrived on the train at Banff only months after the outbreak of the war along with two of his older sisters. Another sister and brother, old enough to enlist at that time, were in the WAAF and RAF respectively and Robin grew up in the Northeast seeing little or nothing of them or of his parents either. The latter, as did so many, visited their children once or twice in the year, but even that died out as time wore on and his father died of a heart attack while the boy was up in the north.

As a wee boy just starting school when he was evacuated, Robin, like so many, has only the sketchiest memories of what decisions and events might have underlain his journey from home then. No memories on his part of any family conference such as Tom and I had experienced, or of the details of his departure from home remain. Only the typical arrival off the train, to be taken for a cup of tea from an urn and a "softie" roll in Trinity Church hall before allocation to his first "foster home".

Thankfully he was not parted from his two elder sisters, Ella and Chrissie, who had accompanied him and with whom I and some of my pals had later played in various backyards. They themselves were even older than I was so were seen as hugely experienced in the ways of the world. After all, were they not sophisticates from our Capital city? But it often felt to me as if they were in a strange way "different" from most of the other evacuees who, we were convinced, were really just transients and we never played with them in quite the same involved way. Whatever it was that we sensed, all three of that detached family were to continue through school in Banff, find careers and marry and have family in or about their adoptive town. In due course their lives became indissoluble from those of the people round them and a return to Edinburgh at the end of the war never happened.

One of the features of their experience was that they had two short stays with different caring families on their first arrival before settling with his final "foster-mother", with whom Robin himself at least maintained contact for over twenty years until he set up home himself when he married. The husband of the second of the families with whom they were billeted had a small boat and through him they sometimes found their way to Peterhead where he was a Chief Coastguard. It struck them as a great irony of the times that they had fled from Edinburgh, which was thought most likely to be bombed, only to experience quite a brisk bombing attack on Peterhead during their holiday there and also a further episode in Banff when Duff House, then a POW camp was also badly damaged by bombing!

Just as the school had played a large part in staffing the early billeting arrangements in 1939 and '40, so also did the Rector of the Academy play a large part in inhibiting any return at the end of the war to their original home near the Royal Mile in Edinburgh. He persuaded them that their schooling would be best completed here - and of course they had settled happily with their "adoptive" mother. In fact, Robin has indicated to me that the permanence of their settlement in Banff gave rise to a conflict that I have not seen remarked on elsewhere in the literature of the effects of wartime evacuation. The problem was the fact that when he was, in due course, to be married up here, he had to decide who was to be "the mother" in the course of the wedding ceremony. His evacuation "Mum" withdrew and it turned out to be his own widowed mother - though he has had some heart searching about this since.

Robin has told me of two features of his early evacuee experience which may not have been general during the war. The first was that he clearly remembers that the local cobbler always repaired and soled and heeled his and his sister's shoes free of charge. The second was that families who kept evacuees for a sustained period of time eventually got a formal letter from King George VI thanking them for their services. The third thing he remarked on, which comforted me greatly since I had thought it peculiar to life in the Manse, was that he and his sisters were relegated to a back room when adult visitors arrived at their home. Small boys were meant to be seen and not heard - or maybe not even seen either!

EVACUATION

Such are the strands of the Celtic Knot so interwoven among those of us from Scotland generally that I only discovered from our recent conversations that Robin's evacuation "mother" was also a nurse on the Red Cross Reserve as my mother had been and that she had nursed the injured in hospital in Banff after the local bombing of Duff House in 1940 alongside my own mother. Thus did one evacuee put down very substantial roots in the town of his adoption so that nearly sixty years from his first arrival he remains here having been schooled, settled in work and married. The label tied to his buttonhole in late 1939 has been well and truly torn off.

The few days surrounding my tenth birthday, on the thirtieth of May, 1940, did not give rise to much celebration. Both my parents were out a lot, my father visiting parishioners whose husbands, sons or brothers were missing or killed during the terrible retreat through France to the Dunkirk beaches, and my mother attending the local hospital where she, as an emergency Red Cross Nursing Sister was preparing the operating theatre and wards for an expected influx of casualties. The paper Swastikas on my wall map in the parlour were now ominously lining the Atlantic shores of NW Europe. Holland and Belgium had just capitulated and we all waited day by day, invasion by German paratroops and a Blitzkrieg by the Luftwaffe.

The sonorous tones of Mr Churchill were listened to as if our very lives depended on them and families crowded round the crackly wireless sets each time his now familiar speeches to Parliament and the Nation both awed and inspired us to face what seemed a desperate situation. In a speech of 27 January in Manchester his rhetoric had roused us from self pity and again, in this tragic early summer, we needed to remind ourselves of his stirring words:

"Come then: let us to the task, to the battle, to the toil - each to   o u r part, each to our station. Fill the armies, rule the air, pour out the munitions, strangle the U-boats, sweep the mines, plough the land, build the ships, guard the streets, succour the wounded, uplift the downcast, and honour the brave....There is not a week, nor a day, nor an hour to lose."

The contrast between Churchill's rumbling sonorities and the prosaic ordinariness of the local newspapers in northeast Scotland at the time was striking. The "Banffie" had always prided itself on wide coverage. There was a whole page of Advertisements on the front, followed by local news, farming prices and mart news, news of the "Rurals" and of the kirks and of the Councils. Europe in June 1940 was crumbling under the onslaught of rampant Nazism before our very eyes but, undeterred, the Editorial in one of the early week's edition of that month, waxed lyrical about the weather:

> "June has come and the glorious appearance of the country in field and wood, on hill and dale, by peaceful hedgerows and quiet country lanes is worthy of the highest traditions of the glowing month".

Most people take the tempo of history from reading books about the relatively remote past. We tend to think of its remorseless march as more of a plod than a sprint, its processes as cumbrous and interwoven with plot and counterplot, action and reaction over years rather than weeks or months. And yet I still find it hard to come to terms with the fact that in the first half of 1940 alone, "history" was being made in front of my very nose at a rate which was almost baffling. In the course of six months, the whole of continental Europe had been put to the sword by the Luftwaffe and Wehrmacht. Austria had been annexed, Poland, Denmark, Holland, Belgium and France had fallen to Hitler's armies. Norway, though claiming neutrality, had been summarily taken over, and worse still, the Maginot Line had simply exemplified the naive military thinking of the French between the wars, was summarily bypassed or simply walked over and the BEF had retreated to the shores of the Channel in the face of overwhelming might. HMS "Hood" and "Royal Oak" had gone to the bottom with a total loss of nearly two thousand good men and only the RAF remained in reasonably good order.

At home, the shelters, the sandbags round the Police station, the coastal defence poles on the beaches and the mines, the air raid warnings and the bombs all created a sense of siege conditions which was wildly at variance with the great traditions of the once all-powerful British Empire which had plastered the maps of a thousand schoolrooms with pink. In those weeks we removed all the railings from round the schools and grand houses to melt them down with the pots and pans spared from innumerable kitchens. They would make armour plate for battleships and body panels for "Spitfires". It was only well after the war had ended that it was revealed that much of the metal taken in the form of railings was brittle cast iron which did not smelt well into anything suitable for munitions.

On Saturdays some of our class went out to the moss near Cornhill or the peat beds near New Pitsligo to collect sphagnum moss to be dried and cleaned to make up into wound dressings for use by the Services and ARP organisations. The Guild ladies and other volunteers then gathered in the church hall (the local depot for this purpose) to clean, sort and pack it.

Another activity of the time was the removal of all road signs lest they make it too simple for invading Germans to find their way around the country. Many of us were sceptical about the significant value of this for we really thought that with their typical Teuton thoroughness, the Germans would have been buying up and copying all the Ordinance Survey maps of the UK for months before war was declared in preparation for their later assault. However, I was inclined to review this attitude some years later when I took my own family on a camping holiday in the south west of Eire. There, it was a favourite ploy of the young bloods to remove or turn round all the rural signposts at crossroads and junctions simply to observe the discomfiture of the tourists who knew no better as they sallied off down the wrong road only to return baffled after a vain journey of indeterminate length. After all, it is only useful to apply oneself to a map if one knows where one is in the first place. As the apocryphal Irishman is alleged to have said when asked by a tourist how to get to, say, Sligo, "Sure now, me bhoy, if I'd been wantin' to go to Sligo, I'd not have started from here at all, at all!"

After the removal of the road signs in and around the town I had watched in ludicrous disbelief as two painters solemnly painted white over the black words (remaining in bold, half-inch high, bas relief) on a white back board proclaiming BANFF BRIDGE STATION. Perhaps the words would not have been seen from 2,000feet but it would not have required Braille to decipher them at ground level! We were then issued with more government Leaflets of Instruction about what to do, and not to do, in the event of invasion. The ringing of all church bells was banned. They would only ever be rung in the event of invasion, probably by parachute or from the sea.

As usual, the "Banffie", with a proper sense of proportion, surrounded such doom-laden notices with reports of the local trade in horses and details of a new Order for the Control of Maggots! Life went on.

The withdrawal from the beaches of Dunkirk began on May 26th, 1940. Operation "Dynamo", as it was called, resulted in all manner of soldiers, sailors and airmen of several nations being picked up by the armadas of Naval and other small boats and ships shuttling across the Dover Straits, many crews repeating the trip under horrendous conditions time and time again until they were literally dropping with fatigue, starvation and fear. Those rescued were decanted on the English side of the Channel just as they stood up - those who could - ragged, wounded, mostly, by then, devoid of their weapons and ammunition. They had dumped all their equipment on the beaches as they struggled out into the sea amidst perpetual machine gunning and bombing to reach anything friendly that floated. Trains then bore them from the ports of the southeast of England to a variety of destinations in the north. Many found their way to the north of Scotland since it was expected that at that time Hitler might make his strike for the UK from Norway or Denmark.

Thus it was that a day or two before my birthday, our house, temporarily devoid of child evacuees, was commandeered by the military to receive about twenty of these adult evacuees - these shattered men. Most were soldiers, but there was at least one airman and a few navymen, although for a day or two it was hard to tell which was which until they were re-equipped with uniforms at the local Territorial Army Drill hall. When they arrived, half clothed in torn, mixed or incomplete and sometimes bloody uniforms, all they wanted to do was sleep. The spare bedrooms and upstairs landing were spread with what mattresses and blankets my mother could find and some extra rations were brought in by an Army truck for the first few days.

Later, Tom and I were allowed to fraternise with the soldiers, mostly, for the sailors and airman were very quickly separated out and whisked away in a truck. We were consequently able to accumulate a much valued collection of regimental cap badges, spent and unused bullets, small pieces of shrapnel, and a variety of brass buttons. A few came directly from the pockets of the soldiers who seemed quite glad to speak to us, although none described in detail the extreme hazards and hardships they had encountered during the past few weeks. Partly this was because they themselves had had insufficient time to recollect in tranquillity the accurate sequence and significance of what had befallen them and partly because much of what they had undergone was not for the ears of small boys.

Nevertheless, one, a certain Jim Steele, a soldier from Belfast, befriended me enough to take us down to the drill hall where he persuaded the Regimental Sergeant Major in charge of re-equipping them to let us have a selection of spare cap badges and brass buttons for our collection. These all had highly inflated bargaining values at school, so I seem to remember that one or another of my parents was frequently called to arbitrate between my brother and myself as to which of us was the true owner of certain of these items.

Soon, however, even the soldiers were re-allocated to Units locally and within a couple of weeks the house was nearly back to normal. The store of peats, sticks and coal in the cellar had taken a beating in that time because of the baths that had been taken by our "visitors". The number of washings of bedding and underwear that my mother and the maid had scrubbed and hung out were countless - though several of the soldiers manfully tried their best to see to their own - and the upstairs rooms and landing were a shambles, though untidy rather than damaged in any way, by the time they departed. After what they had come through we could hardly grudge them that! By the time they had gone, my birthday was forgotten.

The long summer days and short hours of darkness during these months had lead to a reduction in the number of air raid warnings and our descents into "the Black Hole". Germany was thought to be preparing for "Operation Sealion" - the invasion of Great Britiain by sea, and we took the lack of enemy action as ominous rather than as a relief.

CHAPTER 6

BOMBS IN THE MORNING

Within months of the outbreak of war, squads of soldiers, many of the regiment known as The Pioneer Corps, and thought not to be amongst nature's intellectual giants, were to be seen digging and pouring concrete among the trees in front of the Manse, in what had been the grounds of Duff House.

The latter is a magnificent Baroque mansion, which William Duff, Lord Braco, in 1735, commissioned William Adam, one of Scotland's premier architects of the time, to design and build for him as a "magnificent family seat". There is a long plot of dispute and counter dispute between the Duff family and the architect over many years and poor Braco, later to become the first Earl of Fife, never saw the House completed. Nevertheless it came to be recognised as one of the finest and most distinguished 18th century houses in Scotland, one to where Royalty, in the form of the then Prince of Wales, later King Edward VII, would come for a holiday and where many fine treasures of the arts in the form of pictures and furniture could be found. Unfortunately, the Duff family fell on hard times financially and in 1906 the House was given to the people of the two towns of Banff and Macduff. It was in turn a hotel, a sanatorium and a hotel again before the war forced changes on it that neither William Duff nor William Adam might reasonably have foreseen.

In what had been a sylvan pleasance in which the aristocracy had meandered in earlier times, great barbed wire fences with a hard core and grit walkway between them for sentries, materialised around the perimeter of the House and the, by then familiar, corrugated curves of Nissen huts took shape amid the thick belt of trees. Some of the latter around and near the main building were inevitably sacrificed. Machine gun positions, the remains of one of which still form a heap in the rough at the right-hand side of the 13th fairway of Duff House Royal Golf Club, and some searchlights, together with the more subtle positioning of ceramic insulators on the fence poles between the obvious strands of barbed wire confirmed that Duff

House was to become ein Kriegsgefangenenlager - a Prisoner of War camp!

The Pioneer Corps soon gave way to other regiments charged with the probably rather boring task of maintaining a guard and other services over the several hundred German prisoners (including some rather intransigent and arrogant Nazis) who were soon transferred from less permanent camps. The general populace were not encouraged to frequent the Duff House grounds now, although numerous boys like myself would try chatting up either guards or prisoners for "souvenirs" in the way of uniform buttons, expended bullets and bits of shrapnel. As already remarked on, these were always good for swaps for a few marbles, foreign stamps or other war memorabilia up at the school later on.

My father, Rev Dr D Findlay Clark, was then the parish minister of Banff and had been officially appointed as "Officiating Chaplain to the Forces". I still retain his lapel badge of that office which, I think, gave him the equivalent rank of Captain. Since the beginning of the war he had carried out a variety of pastoral services and duties for troops passing through the town and because he spoke and read reasonably good German, the Camp Commandant invited him not only to serve the religious needs of the British soldiers but to act as chaplain to the Germans too. Many were Lutherans, a Protestant sect theologically and liturgically not far from Scottish Presbyterianism. Thus it came about that he became

Duff House refurbished and photographed in 1997. The east wing, formerly on the right of the picture, was virtually demolished by the bombing in 1940.

well known both to many of the guards and the guarded and, because of the pass he held, had rights of fairly free movement (with only some restrictions) throughout Duff House and the surrounding encampment.

As it turned out, there were very few occasions when I was able to enter the camp gates with my father. The demands of school and football had to be reconciled with the opportunities my father had to accompany me on these visits. They were therefore all brief and usually after school on weekdays or on a Saturday afternoon. The latter offered fewer opportunities to talk to the prisoners since it was a time when they had exercise periods outside and most played football. Some, schooled in the Hitler Jugend, did rather self-absorbed callisthenics on a red cinder area which had been the tennis courts in the earlier history of the House as a hotel and sanatorium.

Once into the building I was only permitted to remain in the corridors. There was no entry into the rooms where the prisoners were billeted. My father saw his "parishioners" in a small side room (one of the corner tower rooms) and of course there was a liberal sprinkling of armed British soldiers throughout the House, at the main entrance above the outside staircase, on the landings of the great staircase inside and at smaller doors to the outside. Some of the burgeoning graffiti were no doubt attributable to them, but there were still many in German and no shortage of black Swastikas and "Sieg Heils!" on the plaster walls and door panels. Officially, it was an offence for the prisoners to deface the structure of the building but there were many of them who were still, at that stage of the war, arrogantly Nazi and confident of a prompt and final victory for their side. Unlike many prisoner of war camps, this one held prisoners of both officer and other ranks. The officers always entered by the main doors at the top of the elegantly curved external steps. My father and myself had to "book in" and "out" in a room to the side of the main atrium which seemed to have been used as a kind of office/guardroom.

Even then, however, I was struck by the differences in approach to myself, not only by the prisoners but also by the British guards. Some of the latter, recognising my age, would laughingly offer me a cigarette. As it happened, I only took up the weed when I was twelve (some time after this) and had given it up for good by the time it became legal and I was sixteen. Some of the Germans, whom I had largely expected, from the propaganda pumped out at all of us during the war, to be strutting about in full-dress SS uniforms,

52

snapping their riding crops off their jackboots, were a bit of an anticlimax. Most shuffled around in plimsolls, nondescript olive grey uniform trousers and knitted woollen jerseys. Some were in more recognisable uniforms of olive grey and they transpired to be mostly Luftwaffe aircrew who had been in uniform under their flying suits when shot down. The others, survivors from U-boats or over-adventurous patrols in the north of France, made do with a combination of whatever they had been wearing at the time of their capture and the contents of Red Cross parcels. The coloured patches of bright red, yellow or green cloth sewn on to their outermost garments were simply to identify them as prisoners of war and not, as was a firmly held local belief, aiming points for the guards who might have to shoot at them were they to attempt to escape!

Many had some English and were as keen to try it out on me as I was to pick up some German (which was my father's main motivation for taking me there with him). Some, and I am reluctant to admit it now, eventually began to bore me with pictures and stories about their families. Among the first words I learned after "Guten Tag" and "Aufwiedersehen" were "Kinder" (children), "Frau, Mutter und Vater", (wife, mother and father). Sure enough, after some introductions I would watch them reach for their wallets and hear the familiar, "Ja, hier hab' ich ein Bild..." and out would come the much fingered and dogeared snap of a pleasant enough young woman and one or two usually quite small children. Most of the prisoners were too young to have had older kids.

The guards were reasonably indulgent at these little meetings but seldom themselves went through these rituals. They might have asked me where I lived (or, as Scots say, where I stayed) but they had a job to do and there was always the odd officer or NCO appearing to check that their duties as guards were not being compromised.

In retrospect, I have tried many times to analyse quite what my feelings were about these visits. Ostensibly there to try to learn some German, I was subtly aware of the privilege afforded me to glimpse aspects of wartime life not vouchsafed to the other lads around me. But there was a measure of a strange kind of guilt about it too because I was never able either to tell much about it to my pals nor to boast of how I had given some cheek to Nazis (which I could not ever remember doing anyway). Some of the guilt derived from knowing I was there as a privilege deriving from my father's role. Mostly, however, it derived from the fact that we were all meant, it seemed to us, only to hate Germans and especially Nazi ones, with a burning hatred that would in due course allow us to kill them without compunction. Now I had found out that a goodly proportion of them had boys not unlike myself, missed their families desperately, seemed to enjoy football, sausages and beer just like the Tommies guarding them and none of them seemed in the least inclined to knife me or my father. The Commandant could often be seen chatting amicably with the German senior officer and although some of our lads could be heard referring to "these f*****g krauts", most would greet their charges as Hans or Fritz (whether or not they were Alberts or Helmuts). My concept of "enemy" became a bit muddled by all of this, for a time, at least.

Much of my father's work seemed to involve him in meeting with the Camp Commandant in order to try to get news back to prisoners about their own families in Germany. There were some Italian prisoners in the camp but they were mostly the responsibility of the local Roman Catholic priest. The vast majority of the Germans who had any religious affiliations at all were, as remarked earlier, Lutheran - close enough in doctrine and patterns of worship to Scots Presbyterians for formal church services of either to be virtually indistinguishable - at least to a layman. Some of the more arrogant Nazi prisoners made no attempt to hide their scorn at such of their countrymen as approached my father for help or advice, but on some occasions I could interpret the responses of others as seeming to be half cowed by and half disparaging of these few who were more committed to the Third Reich.

At that stage they probably had to hedge their bets as they could not know how the war was going to turn out. The Nazis among them were sure that Britain would fall to Hitler as the other European countries had in the face of the Blitzkrieg, and soon. Admittedly, 1940 and 1941 were dark days for us Britishers, but Churchill's ringing tones were a marvellous buttress to our confidence. Many was the night we would all press round the wireless to hear his speeches. God help anyone who interrupted while they were being broadcast or who had been foolish enough to let the "wet battery" run down by the overindulgence of listening to Henry Hall and His Orchestra the day before!

But then my visits to Duff House came to an abrupt end. Early one summer morning in July 1940, my brother Tom drew my attention to the characteristic throbbing beat of the BMW engines of a Heinkel 111 bomber. This was before breakfast in the Manse and because my mother was busy in the kitchen downstairs and father was in the bathroom, Tom and I were free to observe. We used that word rather then "watch" because of our aspirations to outdo the Royal Observer Corps post on top of the Hill o' Doune, between the two towns of Banff and Macduff. What we "observed" was this German plane circling over Macduff at no great height in what seemed to us as an unacceptibly leisurely manner. Where were the Spitfires from Dyce? The German plane was now quite low and we could clearly see the black Iron Cross-like insignia on the wings and fuselage.

Then it turned off apparently to drop some incendiaries near the railway station on the hill and on to a fuel storage tank at the foot of the Station Brae. We were a bit ambivalent about this. Banff and Macduff had always been rival towns. Indeed the Earl of Fife had gifted Duff House to both towns jointly in an effort to reconcile the townsfolk of the two Burghs to each other. But Banffers and Macduffers of less mature years had always fought each other (at least during peacetime!). Now this Heinkel seemed to be doing the Macduffers the honour of bombing them first as if they were more important, and anyway, we couldn't see the aircraft properly away over at the other side of the bay. We were quite miffed.

As we watched from an upstairs bedroom window which looked directly over Duff House about 600 yards away, the "Jerry", as we all called them in those days, turned towards us (personally, it seemed) from over and behind Macduff and as the plane was at about 1000 feet we watched the bomb doors open and a stick of bombs wobble out and straighten as they fell towards us. They seemed to fall quite slowly at first but faster and with apparent malice aforethought as they apparently grew in size. We tried to count the bombs as they fell. This school holiday was getting more eventful by the minute.

At that very point my father rushed into the bedroom, half his face smooth and morning fresh and the other half thickly lathered in shaving foam.

"Get down on the floor, you boys!" he bawled, pushing down my shoulders as I reluctantly complied.

"Blast it!" I thought, not inappropriately, a few seconds more and I could almost have seen the bombs explode. Then, "Crrruump, crump, crruump!", as they did. The whole house shook violently and several pictures fell off the wall. I heard my mother cry out, "Daddy, have you got the boys?" or something like that. The windows, however, held fast and no shards of broken glass threatened to decapitate us as they nearly did to some of our neighbours in a couple of houses behind and higher up the hill than ours. Bomb blast had been found throughout the war to do some pretty odd things, but the criss-cross of tape we had so laboriously glued all over the windows at the beginning of the war against just such an eventuality did its stuff.

A great cloud of black smoke and white steam was billowing up from Duff House. It was obvious that it had been hit - and seriously. Then the air raid warning siren went off, a trifle belatedly, and Banff, like a virgin violated in her sleep, began to wake up to the fact that she had been raided. Tom and I wondered whether this had been an attempt to breach the barbed wire fences round the prison camp to allow an escape. On the contrary, it was just another of the bungling errors of wartime whereby the enemy plane's crew had seen the morning guard changing, had thought that the building and its surrounding Nissen huts were a British military base and had let go their bombs rather than cart them all back to Norway or wherever they had set out from. They were probably lost anyway.

Only later did we learn that the bomber turned after hitting Duff House and then dropped five more high explosives on Macduff. The first smoke had simply been from incendiaries of the first "stick" lining up for the high explosives which hit Duff House. But then the cloud of smoke began to rise more vigorously from the battered fuel tank, and, as we discovered later, from the old slaughterhouse in Macduff. We had not seen the incendiaries, much smaller than the high explosive bombs, fall.

BOMBS IN THE MORNING

Within minutes the telephone rang. My mother, who had been a trained nursing sister and midwife (though that aspect of her training had little relevance now) was on the Red Cross Reserve and she was to attend at Chalmers Hospital in the town immediately as casualties were already on the way. Dr Hugh Smith, the local surgeon, had already been advised and the other general practitioners were being sought also. The news was that at Duff House some in the main building had been killed but were not yet identified. No prisoners had escaped and the damage had been confined to the House itself and some of the golf course fairways.

Very quickly my mother had changed into her crisp white uniform and dashed off in a taxi to the hospital. We never had a car. We saw little of her for some days for when she was briefly off duty she slept, sometimes at the hospital, and we had to make shift for ourselves. Fortunately the schools were on holiday so there were no deadlines to meet. For a time there was much clanging of ambulance bells and a great commotion around the House, though at that time the trees surrounding it and in front of the Manse on Sandyhill Road were much thicker than now. Nobody other than the Police, the military and the ARP was allowed near the incident.

The whole of the east wing of the building containing the kitchens and the main heating boilers had been so badly damaged that it was later totally, and easily, demolished and blast and shrapnel damage was evident elsewhere about the building. It still is to this day, mainly around the southeast corner and the main external staircase, some of which had to be completely replaced. The first three or four bombs of the stick fell short of the building and blew craters in the hallowed ground of those parts of Duff House Royal Golf Club not yet dug up for agricultural purposes. Two of them were never filled in since they were in a useful position to entrap a pulled drive from the seventeenth tee and the holes remain to this day as grassy bunkers, enhanced and dug out a bit more to tidy them up by local golfers and later much visited during the blackout by courting couples and oftener, and to perhaps more futile purposes, by generations of golfers.

The six Germans killed, (and two British - cooks, I think) were later buried by my father at a brief service at the cemetery. Later, the bodies were exhumed for repatriation to Germany. There were many injured, however, about thirty or forty as I remember, and some very severely. My mother told me that some had been blown into the disintegrating boiler and were not only wounded by shrapnel but were burned by steam and were full of glass from the water tubes inside the boiler.

Stories about the morning's events, some perhaps apocryphal, but others with the ring of truth, abounded. The first told of how the two worthy lads in the Royal Observer Corps dugout on top of the Hill o' Doune had reported in to the Fighter Command airfield at Dyce, near Aberdeen, just over forty miles away, with increasing tones (and words) of urgency about the enemy bomber - only to be disbelieved on the grounds that there was nothing in Banff worth bombing.

The conversation on the field telephone might have gone thus:

"Hello, hello! Is that Dyce? - Aye. Weel, there's a Jerry Heinkel fleein' ower Banff an' Macduff" (Pause)

"Aye, this is the ROC observer on the Hill o' Doune". (Pause)

"Aye, aye min, we're sure. We can bloody near see in his cockpit - aye, there's a Swastika on his tail". (Pause)

"Aye, he's bin here for a filie. Could ye nae get somebody up tae shot 'im doon?" (Pause)

"God Almichty, min, ah ken there's a bloody war on. Bit there's mair o' it here the noo than there is in Aiberdeen" (Pause)

"Fit wye should Ah ken fit he's seein' tae boomb in Banff. Jist pit up a Spitfire". (Pause)

"Jesus, min, he's openin' his boomb doors noo. Get bloody movin'!

(Loud explosions from left centre)

"Noo d'ye believe me. He's drappin' his boombs noo. Ye can hear them ga'an aff or ye must be deef!"

At this point the threshold of credibility on the part of the local Fighter Controller at Dyce seemed to have been reached and rapid action ensued. The bomber was apparently intercepted some miles off the east coast as it headed east and shot down, with the loss, some said, of two of the crew of three. The second, and almost certainly apocryphal, story then circulated was that the pilot, who was picked up from his rubber dinghy in the North Sea, hearing that he had bombed and killed some of his own men, then went mad.

Of course, censorship of the press and other media was strict throughout the war and it was an inflexible rule that no names of towns or cities were ever reported in relation to bombings or other military events lest the enemy get useful feedback. Consequently, the account of that morning's events in the "Banffshire Journal" of 23 July 1940 reads much more blandly (and proved to be less than accurate). It ran:

"Raider Bombs NE Towns
Some Casualties"

"One or two were killed and some seriously injured when a single enemy aircraft bombed a northeast town yesterday morning.

Four heavy bombs were dropped after the raider had circled the district for some time. Local ARP services assisted the wounded to hospital.

Immediately afterwards the raider dropped five high explosive and a number of incendiary bombs on a neighbouring town. None of the explosives did any damage apart from making a crater on a road and slightly damaging one building on the outskirts of the town.

All the incendiaries dropped in gardens and other open spaces and were quickly extinguished without starting any fires.

Fighter aircraft appeared and chased the raider out to sea."

There was another rather entertaining, and true, story of that morning told me, more recently, by a Mrs Meldrum who was, like my mother, a Red Cross member engaged in the nursing of the wounded from that incident. She was herself cycling down the road not far from Duff House at the time of the bombing and was probably nearer the actual blasts than we were.

She told how, in the absence of my father who was using his

German at the House itself and therefore not available at the hospital, a young student who had been studying languages was hastily recruited to act as an interpreter for the German wounded. She happened to be the sister of a local lawyer's son who was later to become a well known novelist and film script writer, Neil Paterson, author of, among other things, "The China Run" and "Behold Thy Daughter". The wounded were all taken quickly to the hospital about a mile away from the POW camp where they were all lying around the wards and corridors of the hospital on beds and stretchers until the priority cases could be ascertained and dealt with in the treatment rooms and operating theatre.

With the doctor, surgeon and nurses listening intently and posing the questions to be asked of patients, this young girl patiently went from one to the other speaking quietly in German to ascertain their injuries, whether they were in pain, and so forth. This went on well until they came to one who utterly failed to respond to any of the questions in clear German and simply blinked uncomprehendingly no matter how the young lass varied her German phraseology. One of the doctors then said,

"Well, just ask him once more if he knows how long he's been here and how he feels."

At which point the patient immediately brightened up and declared,

"Ah'm a fairmer fae oot the road. Ah've been here for a fortnicht wi' ma hernia an' ah'm deein' jist fine!"

It may be hard for readers now to grasp how intense was the propaganda generated in the civilian community as part of the war effort. In schools and public places, large posters depicted Nazi soldiers and SS men as violent, malevolent beasts bent on rape and pillage, regardless of all the tenderer human emotions. They were drawn as harsh, jackbooted criminals striding with wicked expressions and fixed bayonets over weeping children and cowering civilians. There were, of course, some like that. That was the trouble. We were reminded by equally lurid posters that "Walls had Ears" and that "Careless Talk Costs Lives" because of the need to be on guard against Fifth Columnists and spies. Again, though few came within the ambit of our experience, there were some of both, even in the rural northeast.

BOMBS IN THE MORNING

"Lord Haw Haw" (William Joyce) and his traitorous broadcasts were the object of ridicule, though every now and again there might just be a sneaking doubt that some of what he claimed as magnificent German victories might just be true. Occasionally, his curiously nasal and whining voice would come through the earphones of my crystal set with the bedframe aerial announcing some great Nazi advance, news of which, in modified form, would be reported by the BBC next day. Then, as now, the truth had to be sifted from a variety of sources and most people, though favouring the BBC and Winston Churchill, filled out their grasp of events from newspapers, discussion with friends and snippets from the letters of their relatives who were actually in the war situation at home or abroad. In this context, the Allied propaganda countered with the generation of attitudes, by posters and inference from what was reported, that the only good German was a dead German.

It therefore came as something of a surprise when I first made closer acquaintance with some of these self-same Germans. For some weeks my mother nursed the most severely wounded prisoners in the wards of Chalmers Hospital while the guards patrolled the corridors with their rifles. When, on Sunday afternoons, at the instigation of my parents, I visited these poor men covered in bandages it seemed ironic that they had to have sentries guarding them. The poor devils could hardly move on their beds much less contrive "The Great Escape". The guards thought so too. One needs to bear in mind that in those days there were no antibiotics and sepsis was a much greater risk than it is now. The injuries these men suffered, and especially the burns, were life threatening. In one case my mother told me she had, both in theatre and in the ward, with scalpel and tweezers, extracted from one man's body alone, 365 pieces of glass and shrapnel, some several inches long. She remembered it because there was one for every day of the year and at the start of that endeavour the man was not then expected to survive, or even to see the next day.

I remember him, Herbert Büschel, well; pale, weak and moaning gently until many days later he was able to sit up and begin to recover. His name, with those of many others, is to this day in my mother's autograph book. "Meiner fursorglichen Pflegemutter meinem herzlichsten Dank fur die aufopfernde Pflege, die ich nicht vergessen werde. - Herbert Büschel, Gittersee uber Dresden,

Birkigterstrasse Rang 64" (To my exceptionally caring "care mother" or ward sister, my heartfelt thanks for the outstanding care which I will never forget)

Herbert had initially not been expected to live for even a day or two, so serious were his external and internal injuries. Although he gave an address in Dresden, we never knew whether he had any family there. On our last visit to the ward before all the Germans were moved away he called me over and asked me to take a memento in thanks for what my mother had done for him in hospital. He could speak little or no English but my father and I understood his German enough to

Many thanks for the good treatment. Never I will forget all the good, what I have get here. GOTT save your house all days. All the best for you, your husband and your children.

Walter Anders
Bremen
Meyerstr. 161

Vielen Dank für die aufopfernde Pflege, die ich nie vergessen werde.

Ernst Goethling
Segeletz/Neustadt a. d.
Dosse-Fam

Für die aufopfernde Pflege sage ich der lieben Pflegemutter, Mrs. Findlay Clark, meinen herzlichsten Dank.

Hermann Fisher
Letmathe i. Westf.
Gennastr: 50

Meiner fürsorglichen Pflegemutter meinen herzlichsten Dank für die aufopfernde Pflege, die ich nie vergessen werde.

Herbert Büschel
Gittersee über Dresden
Birkigten Hang

Herzlichen Dank für alles Gute.

wl-Heinz Barkhausen
Germany
emen-Burg, Heerstr. 45.

26. 7. 1940.

Vielen Dank für alles Gute.

Gerhard Flade
Germany
Stettin, Pasewalker Str. 2.

26. 7. 1940.

Samples of the entries made in my mother's autograph book by grateful German POW's whom she had nursed following the bombing of Duff House, Banff.

grasp that the old Iron Cross which he took from his wallet had been his father's from the first World War. It was an overwhelming gift but he would not hear of our returning it to him. I like to think that we have treated that token with the honour it deserves. Many times subsequently, looking at Buschel's Dresden address, did I wonder whether his family, if indeed he had any alive at the time, survived the Allies' firestorm there some years later.

Every Sunday, my father, brother and I would visit these wounded men in the ward. Sometimes my mother would be there on duty and in uniform anyway and it was quite strange to see the professional assurance, gentleness and directness that she demonstrated in going about her business as a nurse. This was an aspect of her that we had never seen in her other roles. She was, if anything, mainly attached to the role of "parish minister's wife" and then "mother of two boys". Here, however, she was a different person, proud of her profession and operating comfortably within the terms of her long training and experience as a nurse and midwife. She had nothing to prove in that role and, I think, was the better for

But as for our interaction with the POW's, father would talk to them in German and I would try my few words. To one, Walter Anders, who was a Luftwaffe pilot from Bremen, I was persuaded by my parents to donate the two sided mouth organ which I had got for my birthday not many weeks before. He at least could play it, something I had not then mastered. I passed it, a Hohner, made in Germany, to him somewhat reluctantly, unaware of the irony. His gratitude was all too obvious. He took it quietly, thanked me warmly and began to play "Die Lorelei". As he did so, his eyes rested the while on the small snapshot of his young wife and children on the locker by his bedside. The ward fell silent as all, Germans and British alike, listened and watched as Walter's eyes dampened as he played and one or two hummed the tune with him. As the last plaintive notes died there were several others sniffing back a tear and I wondered again whether for a second time in this wretched war my "weakness" had been spotted by anyone else.

He had some English and his entry in my mother's autograph book reads: "Many thanks for the good treatment. Never will I forget all the good, what I have get here. GOTT save your house all days. All the best for you, your husband and your children. - Walter

Anders, Bremen, Meyerstrasse 161." There were others, writing in equally plaintive but grateful tones. For they too had been subject to their own side's propaganda and had previously thought that the British would not bother to care for them when there were simultaneously other British casualties.

After the bombing, Duff House was run down as a POW camp and the surviving prisoners were shipped, I believe, to Canada where they stayed until the end of the war. Repaired, and still with the fences in position, it became a base for many regiments of troops throughout the war. Poles, even a few Free French, several British regiments including large numbers of the King's Own Scottish Borderers (the Kosbies as they were affectionately known - particularly to the girls!) the Highland Light Infantry and the Argyll and Sutherland Highlanders and eventually the 42nd Norwegian Mountain Brigade all inhabited the building - richly enhancing its graffiti and some of its traditions, though seriously eroding its original decor and grace. Most of the graffiti and drawings on the plaster, from what I remember of them during my visits had the harshness, the sexuality and sometimes the wit of frustrated men *en masse*. Some, however, had a sense of history and of the period and others of pride in their task and of their nationality. It has been possible to renovate the building and yet to preserve some trace of that troubled history.

Perhaps now, having opened as a Country House Gallery and containing fittings and pictures worthy of its period and style, Duff House can recover something of its original Adam majesty and show off that great facade and staircase to an increasing number of admirers who, when they wander through the gallery rooms and corridors, may ponder not only on the longer story but also on some of the more recent history from only half a century ago encapsulated in this historic and noble pile.

CHAPTER 7

BANGS AND DRAMS

Although the bombing of Duff House held significant drama in that people were actually killed and wounded in numbers and the sequelae rumbled through the town for months afterwards, the other main bombing attack of the war on Banff occurred in high summer just over a year later.

My parents were at a wedding at which my father had officiated on Saturday afternoon 16 August 1941. It was described in the "Banffshire Journal" (my favourite local archive) of 19 August 1941 as a "pretty Naval wedding" of Paymaster-Lieutenant J Scot RNVR to Miss Jessie Strath in Trinity Church, Banff (not at his own Parish Church of St Mary's, because the two respective ministers covered for each other during two summer holiday months). Thereafter there was a reception at the Fife Arms Hotel, where, no doubt, they were in convivial mood throughout the other alcohol loaded episode about to be described. In the course of my parents' celebrations, I was left free in the Manse to spend the afternoon as I liked.

From the back garden I heard the sound of a German plane and soon after caught a glimpse of what looked like a Junkers JU88 crossing over the bay quite low and heading toward Whitehills, the next village a couple of miles away. Keen to miss nothing exciting, I jumped on my bike and pedalled furiously up over the Whinhill to see better from a higher viewpoint what was afoot. There had been no air raid siren at this point but the sudden explosions were unmistakable and a column of smoke soon rose from the direction of the links.

The air raid siren actually sounded as I pedalled my bicycle over the hill toward the action and I watched as the German fighter/bomber made another strafing run over Boyndie Distillery on the west side of the town. Machine guns rattled and I saw the AFS (Auxiliary Fire Service) van and trailer speeding out along Victoria

Place. It was a curious situation at the distillery. The product of the place in very potent form was still in vats and barrels while the grain lofts had become billets for soldiers. It was presumably the sight of some of the latter which had triggered the aggression of this wandering intruder.

Several lone German planes would wander close in to the coast from time to time. They were as often lost and looking for a fix from a landmark or from the shore line as they were reconnoitering the coast for new airfields or military installations. No decent German officer, knowing his Schnapps, could have had such an ill regard for good Scotch as to initiate such a heathen waste of the good stuff! On the other hand, he may have reckoned that Allied morale would suffer disproportionately were he to destroy the "water of life" on such a scale.

As I freewheeled down the seaward side of the Whinhill, I caught sight of the local Police Sergeant pedalling equally fast, though with more apparent effort, toward Inverboyndie. Other than his curiosity, a few conditions had to be satisfied by his presence at the scene. First, the site of firefighting operations had to be secured from casual sightseers and others. Second, the possible loss of life and incidence of injuries had to be established and recorded for posterity in the dog-eared notebook in his breast pocket. Thirdly, and most important perhaps to the Law, was that a certain local slater and tiler, well known to be more than partial to "the cratur", was a member of the fire fighting team, and was, at that very moment, in the act of scooping or attempting to scoop, with his tin hat, the neat spirit from the surface of the burn into which countless gallons of the stuff had leaked as a result of the German's war effort.

Meanwhile the JU88 came round again, this time to the accompanying stutter of a couple of Lewis guns hastily manned by the discomfited soldiery, and dropped a stick of incendiaries to finish off the work begun with high explosives on the first run. None of the now numerous spectators seemed to be aware that the German was also shooting at them, or at least in their general direction, although several other boys and myself were quickly able to acquire still hot spent bullets from the banks of earth near the distillery dam and from the field by the burn. At this point the Luftwaffe retreated eastwards at low altitude and high speed, thereby missing all the fun.

There was a degree of confusion while all this was happening. Flames could be seen rising amid the smoke from the grain loft and warehouses and while firemen ran out hoses and the soldiers who were not away in the town off-duty shifted arms and ammunition, "volunteers" from among the adult spectators were also equipping themselves as best they could at a moment's notice for the task before them. No doubt there was some equivocation about what that task's priorities were. For myself, the whole thing had an immediacy which the bombing of Duff House had lacked. Only yards separated me from all that was going on until the police and an Army officer cleared all of us not engaged officially from the scene.

In other books about the Blitz in London, writers have on a number of occasions remarked, not only on the gruesome, odd or frightening sights they came across after and during a bombing raid, but also on the strange smells that prevailed. On the scale of events in the major cities when they were bombed, of course, there must necessarily have been sewers ruptured, chemical factories and even chemists' shops blown apart and strange materials burned. And, often, the tragic smell of death, both of animals and of humans.

There was nothing of the latter at Inverboyndie; but that afternoon, for a period before the fresh wind blew them out to sea, a strange admixture of smells filled the air. Initially there was the characteristic rather acrid smell of cordite and high explosive mingling with the smoke from the machine gun fire. That soon was overlain by a dusty, sharp smell of disintegrated stonework and mortar, and that in turn mixed with the almost fresh smell of dry mature timbers burning as the rafters and old wooden floors caught the flames. Capping all of these, however, was the overwhelming bouquet of a fine malt whisky as the almost water-clear spirit poured down over the field and into the burn.

True to form, Mr Jamieson, our Sunday School Superintendent and the local joiner and undertaker (for these were the occupational priorities, in descending order of importance, I, at my age then, accorded him) had been shorthanded in his firefighting tasks to the extent that our slater and tiler was dogged in his attempts, with several others, out of uniform, to salvage more of the 120 proof nectar so desperately running to waste. His concentration at the burn side, while the fire raged on in the grain lofts, was seriously disturbed, however, by the firmness with which the Police Sergeant felt his collar. It was an arresting moment.

Then followed a vigorous discussion between the Bobby and the Fire Chief as to whether it was more important for Mr S to resume, however unsteadily, his duties as a fireman, or for the law to take its course and for him to jog, handcuffed to the Police bicycle, and charged with the looting of whisky from bonded property, along to the jail on Reidhaven Street where, at that very moment, the siren attached to its highest point, was sounding the "All Clear".

The "Banffshire Journal" of 19 August 1941, though hampered by the wartime rule that no place subjected to enemy action could be named in a newspaper, allowed itself a column on that afternoon's events. The Northeast's edition of "Whisky Galore" was every bit as entertaining as Compton McKenzie's novel, and variations on the theme - as well as exaggerations of it - were worked locally for months afterwards. The "Banffie", as it is called locally, described events thus:

"Sneak Raider in North-East
Looting Charge in Sheriff Court

A few men who got "dead" drunk on bombed whisky were the only "casualties" when a single enemy aircraft made a sneak raid over and around a North-East of Scotland town on Saturday afternoon and dropped high explosive bombs on a warehouse which caught fire and was burned to the ground.

Thousands of gallons of whisky in casks were lost either by burning or running to waste over the land in the vicinity, and so overpowering were the results that even farm animals grazing in the neighbourhood became visibly intoxicated.

Happily, nobody was injured in the raid even though the raider machine-gunned part of the district after dropping his bombs.

BANGS AND DRAMS

The German High Command communique of Sunday stated:- "In the struggle against Great Britain a successful day attack of the Luftwaffe was directed against armament factories in Northern Scotland"

Machine Gunned

The aircraft flew low over the town and was seen by hundreds of people in the streets. A number of people also saw and heard the bombs falling and only then realised it was an enemy plane. After releasing his bombs the raider circled over the district and town and at one point opened fire with his machine guns, but, fortunately, no one was hit by bullets, although there were some narrow escapes. Two fire brigades from the town and scores of other helpers fought the blaze at the warehouse for many hours and it was completely extinguished before darkness fell. Streams of burning whisky flowed among the grass fields in the vicinity. A nearby cottage suffered some slight damage by blast and had some of its windows blown in but no one was injured. The occupant, Mr John McDonald, was actually standing at his door watching the plane, unaware it was an enemy raider when he saw the bombs released and witnessed the explosion which seemed to send debris into the air as high as the plane itself.

Whisky Theft Charge

A sequel to the occurrence yesterday was the appearance in custody at a North Scottish Sheriff Court of a member of a fire brigade, WGS, slater, aged 42, on a charge of having on Saturday, at a warehouse forming part of premises which had been subjected to attack by enemy aircraft, stolen a quantity of proof whisky, contrary to the Defence (General) Regulations, whereby he was liable to imprisonment for a term not exceeding twelve months.

He pleaded guilty.

The Procurator Fiscal stated that accused was a member of a fire brigade which was called to a fire at a warehouse resulting from bombing by enemy aircraft, when casks of whisky were involved. Some men were engaged in bursting casks to prevent the fire from spreading, allowing the contents to run away. Accused, who was nearby on duty, held out his hat and gathered some of the whisky and drank it. Later he was seen to be in a hopeless condition of drunkenness and was lying on a grass bank not far away when he was apprehended by the police.

An agent appearing on the accused's behalf stated that accused had had nothing to eat for some time before he was called on duty as a member of the fire brigade. Owing to the terrific heat and strong smell of whisky he felt somewhat overcome and took a little of the whisky that was being poured away, thinking it would revive him a little. He did not realise the whisky was too strong to be taken nor did he realise he was stealing it when it was actually being poured on the ground. If all stories were true, even some cows and sheep in the neighbourhood had been imbibing too freely from the whisky on the ground, but fortunately for them, they were not subject to the jurisdiction of the Court.

First Case

This was the first case of the kind in the district concerned and it appeared some other people had been at the same "game" as accused, although they would probably not appear in Court. He asked the Court to take into consideration that the theft was committed quite unthinkingly and that the little whisky accused tasted was actually being thrown away at the time.

The Sheriff said that he did not wish anything that was said or done in that case to cast any doubt on the seriousness of a conviction for looting under the Defence Regulations. The penalties laid down under the Regulations showed how seriously such offences were regarded in the ordinary case. The offence to which the accused had pleaded guilty was in the circumstances only a technical case of looting, because what he took was beyond the stage of being any use to its owners or anyone else. At the same time it was a serious offence, particularly for a man engaged, as accused was at the time, in the civil defence services, and conduct of that kind could not be passed over lightly.

He imposed a penalty of £3 or 10 days' imprisonment, and allowed a week for payment of the fine."

So ran the official view of the episode. The reality was closer to the hinted-at view of the accused's agent when he declared that others, not coming before the Court, had been at the same game. Stories, true and apocryphal, were legion. The notion of bursting the casks in order to prevent them exploding, was considered a brainwave of "altruism" on the part of another fireman and this task seemed to be carried on much longer than the extent of the blaze might have warranted. Several firm axe blows could be heard a while after the last flames had been dowsed. It needed a little time to organise, with appropriate stealth, and the willing help of "interested bystanders", containers more secure than service tin hats to retain one or two samples for any future "investigation".

There were some questions asked too about the time it took to set up return of fire against the German plane - and the accuracy of it when it was set up. Perhaps it had been the effect of the fumes - or something! Perhaps too it was no more than coincidence that my father, quietly partial to a drop o' the "Auld Kirk", was offered, and accepted, a number of pleasantly potent drams on his visiting rounds about the town in the months that followed a period of significant austerity.

As for the animals, even before the attacker was long out of sight to the east, ducks on the mill dam adjacent, and in the burn that ran from it into the sea, were in such a state of euphoria that they were quacking and scuttering about erratically, and, sadly, in under an hour, some became so befuddled with alcohol that, swimming in the burn, they put their heads down to sup some more and succumbed, later to be washed down to the sea where they were found dead next day. A number of ewes and first year lambs had become somehow less sheepish and a bit noisier than usual. Two cows, when I returned to the scene later that evening, were "moo-ing" out of harmony and having great difficulty standing or walking. It is said that the farmer could not milk them for days. Whether that was because, some said, their milk tasted of good malt whisky, or whether it was that they became just too skittish to catch, or whether the farmer became too skittish to catch, remains a mystery.

The whole episode, perhaps because it occurred on a fine summer Saturday afternoon, when people might have been watching a football match, doing a bit of shopping, attending weddings and so forth, carried an air of slight unreality - even seeming like a sort of entertainment. When Duff House had been bombed there had been a suddenness and a somberness about it occasioned by the loss of life and serious injury which was quite unlike the comedy of errors enacted at the distillery.

The time and the topography of the place led to the ground and roads round the distillery becoming a natural viewing gallery regardless of the police's best efforts. They were few and we were many. The incentive to prevent, by any means, fair or foul, too severe a wastage of the "free spirit" was great. Poor Mr S was just unlucky that his reputation had preceeded him to the site, and although the press report said that the fire had been put out by nightfall, what it really meant was that it had **not** been put out **until** nightfall!

The reason for that was that the so-called preventive rupturing of the barrels distracted good men from beating and hosing out the flames. It was amazing how many axe-smashed barrel tops and how few axe-smashed side staves of barrels were found washed down the burn to the beach next day! Perhaps it was just easier to strike down on the tops than it was to swing an axe sideways. There were also numerous lengths of stirrup pump hose and metal piping about a foot long with pieces of stick corking the ends to be found in bins and ditches for a time. They fitted the rule pocket of a boiler suit or dungarees, or the inside of a Wellington boot perfectly!

It has also seemed a great shame that the solicitor who defended the accused was never named. His ingenuity and persuasiveness in trying to mitigate his client's misdemeanour was such that he might have expected many more commissions to defend others in court. The fire brigade certainly never had such a stimulating occasion at any other time until perhaps VE night in May 1945.

Spectators continued to arrive at the scene on the following Sunday, ostensibly to look at the damage, but hoping nevertheless that somewhere there might be a forgotten little puddle of something that was neither rain nor hose water. On foot, on bicycles and even in buses they continued to turn up for a day or two of that week, to view the "tragic" scene and to vie with each other in telling tales of mice and men on that famous Saturday which began in solemn truth and ended in hilarity a good few jumps beyond veracity.

It was hard not to feel a little sorry for the German bomber crew who were so keen to return home in time for tea. They never knew what they missed - in both senses. Perhaps the ultimate irony of fate is that the remaining parts of the distillery were demolished in 1986/7 and in the latter year, all that was left went up in flames by accident. The fire brigade could do nothing to save it!

CHAPTER 8

ON THE HOME FRONT

Those desperate years of a siege economy and way of life while the fate of our country - and indeed of all of Western democracy - was being decided on the beaches of Dunkirk, and later in the air over the southern counties of England by the "First of the Few" were years of hardship for everybody. Later generations might find it hard to grasp that the stringencies of rationing of food and clothing not only made huge demands on the ingenuity of mothers as housekeepers but also made what financial resources one had seem largely irrelevant to the way of life.

We were all levelled by our 10pence worth of meat per week, our two ounces of butter or margarine, the great paucity of most fruits and, so far as we children were concerned, our two, or later, four ounces of sweets per week. Everyone was urged by poster campaigns, radio and newspapers to "Dig for Victory!". The golf course was dug up and planted with potatoes and oats. Everyone howked and tilled spare pieces of ground, erstwhile herbaceous borders and flower beds to grow lettuces, carrots, turnips, potatoes and brassicas so vital to augment the minimal supplies in the shops. Bread was made with a high proportion of wheat husk and became gradually darker. Coffee and tea, both imported at a high cost in the lives of merchant seamen, were very scarce and even milk and eggs were strictly rationed.

Oddly, it is one of the great ironies of life that only recently has research into the appalling record of heart and circulatory disease among Scots people shown that the very generation which endured these privations is now better able to resist the damaging effects of over rich and over fatty feeding because of the enforced high fibre, vegetable-rich, low meat, low sugar diet of wartime.

In North Scotland, we were privileged in that many people had access to farmland and farmers as well as to very generous fishermen. Theoretically, the police were obliged to be on the watch for "black market" transfer of eggs, butter, the odd pheasant or brace

R.B.1
16
MINISTRY OF FOOD
1953-1954
SERIAL NO.
AP 551813

RATION BOOK

Surname STEPHEN Initials J.A.
Address 19 Drumochli Pk

IF FOUND RETURN TO ANY FOOD OFFICE

F.O. CODE No.
Sc.E1

NATIONAL REGISTRATION
IDENTITY CARD

The Ration Book and the personal Identity Card held by everyone during the war. The latter could be demanded to be seen at any time by anyone with the appropriate authority e.g. Police or the military.

of partridges or pigeons from the back of a "fairm chiel's" bike to a back door or shopping basket.

In practice, however, it was impossible and largely impractical for the long arm of the law to reach out after every such transaction, especially in the face of the great ingenuity exercised by most exponents of the trade. To the writer's knowledge this was never more than a "cottage industry", a small scale mutual support system often within families and close friends and far removed from the large scale swindles and sharp practices of the so-called "spivs" toward the end of the war in the urban communities. In any case, there was a certain amount of goodwill among neighbours and friends which allowed of mutual collaboration. If someone had a farming relative and another knew a fisherman, then it was obvious that each might benefit reciprocally.

Long before my mother's own quest for a source of fresh

eggs, my father and she had faithfully visited a bedbound old farmer in a hamlet about three and a half miles away who was unable to rise from his bed because of back injuries. His wife and family had, however, kept some farming enterprises going and it was to that lonely establishment that my mother would frequently despatch me for a dozen of the valuable ovoids.

Nowadays no self respecting mother would send her ten year old son to walk alone on country roads, summer and winter, in daylight or darkness, in fair weather or foul for a dozen eggs - or indeed for anything! It galled me that so often I would hear the shout: "David, Here's the money. Take a run out to old Mr D's and get a dozen eggs," on a Saturday morning just as I would be getting my football boots for a game in the park. The proposal that I could go later in the day cut no ice with that formidable lady. As an ex-Ward Sister in Dundee Royal Infirmary during the first World War she knew what command was all about.

And so it would be that I would set out on the long trail, the first mile on good main road to the Milesteen Briggie and then up past the farm, through cawing rooks and bosky shadows of the Craw Widdie and on to the Alvah turn.

The next section was good arable land, well husbanded and fenced and holding fewer subtle fears for a young mind. But the final stretch up the hill and past the kirkyard at Alvah was a tough one. There were ghosties at night or in the gloom of a winter snowstorm, but in the summer the threat was from the schoolmaster's dog, a huge and menacing Great Dane, none too well controlled, which habitually guarded the approaches to the village by standing watching the road with fore paws perched on a huge pile of sheeps' skulls as it barked malevolently. Among these whitening relics I firmly believed there to be the skulls of previous small boys who had wandered by chance along that empty road.

In the shadows of the woods a whistled tune or two had sufficed to keep terror at bay, but now there was a dryness in my thrapple, and anyway a whistle would probably have brought the great brute lunging in my direction. There was never a soul there when I needed company. I later found out that the schoolmaster fed his hound on boiled whole sheep's heads and that no schoolboys were missing.

ON THE HOME FRONT

Old Mr D was, of course, an invalid always in his bed when I would be ushered into the room to have a conversation of sorts with him while the lady of the house busied herself to get me a glass of milk and some oatcakes to sustain me on the return journey. Small boys find such a situation with adults a bit of a strain but I always did my best to be polite and interesting to them, perhaps to fend off the evil powers that might assault me on the way home. The eggs, of course, were of superb quality, free-range, we would call them now, and they were much enjoyed later.

As I grew older and got a bike, the whole operation became easier and quicker, but in the course of several such ventures there were more than a few quickenings of the heartbeat, especially in the winter when I might have set out in the dark after school on a Friday to avoid having to go on Saturday. That really was creepy. Hoolets would call from the darkness and there would be scuttlings from the undergrowth. An eye of a stirk would suddenly catch the moonlight or a sheep would cough like the death rattle of an old man. Trees that I might have climbed with a glad heart during the day held all sorts of menace in their tangled and creaking branches and none of that would be relieved by even the passing of a single car or sight of a single citizen.

In winter, I pulled my sledge all the way knowing that if there were more uphill sections on the way out, then at least there were some great long runs downhill on the way back. Then, of course, all the cars and folk that were never seen when I needed them would appear to hinder my snowy progress. The box of a dozen eggs too tended to inhibit my normal elan with the sledge or bike.

By a quirk of fate, my elder daughter and son-in-law now live within a stone's throw of the cottage to which I travelled all these long years ago. It has taken some time for the reflex frisson of apprehension I used to feel on the hill past the kirkyard to dissipate in the face of a series of happier visits. The schoolmaster, his dog and the sheep's heads have all disappeared.

If an egg supply was thus maintained at some cost of nervous energy, a supply of fresh fish necessitated only a mile and a half's walk to the harbour at Macduff. Off-shore fishing, because of minefields (friendly and hostile) and the risk of attack from air and sea, was also limited and many of the larger boats had been commandeered to act as minesweepers and fleet auxiliaries, Motor Fishing Vessels (MFV's) as they came to be called.

Nevertheless, we youngsters were often, especially during the summer holidays, to be found fishing for rock cod or pollack (saithe) from the rocks or piers at the harbours and it was easy for us to congregate on the quayside as the boats came in and to shout, "Hey min, gie's a fry!". The fishers were never slow to throw up a dozen or so herring or mackerel to each boy even as they went about their business of landing the catch.

Many's the day my brother and my pals and I would head for home from Macduff with a substantial meal for the whole family threaded on our fingers or with a bit of fishing line through the silver gills of these fine fish. It was to the great credit of these fishermen that they never discriminated between boys from Banff or boys from Macduff in spite of the rivalry between the towns. Naturally my mother would pretend to some shock that I, a minister's son, should demean myself by "begging" as she put it. I myself felt no such scruples for seeking the gifts we were never grudged and I noted that, for all the times I brought fish home, they were never wasted. If anything else did happen to be ready for the tea it would be put aside for another time and the frying pan and oatmeal soon put to work on the herring and mackerel.

The more obvious difference between these days and now would, however, be not so much observed in feeding habits (which, after all, were always more private anyway) as in clothing styles. As young schoolboys we were limited to one pair of boots, one pair of black plimsolls, one pair of trousers for school and everyday and one pair "for good" together with perhaps a couple of shirts, two pairs of pants and two vests, a pullover for winter and perhaps a jacket or corduroy blouson with a front opening zip.

These had to last a year. It was a far cry from the shell suits, trainers, designer clothes and huge variety of styles and garments now not only available but actually worn, sometimes just for a few months before being discarded in favour of new and better styles. A year or two before the war my brother and I had been kitted out in full Highland kilt gear - bottle green serge jackets with silver buttons, Balmoral bonnets, stockings, sporrans and buckled shoes - the lot! That had to last a long time - and it did. All our workaday and school clothes were for several years, much darned and patched and there were many rows about our behaving improperly in inappropriate clothes. Tree climbing, for crows' eggs and the like, sliding on the skating pond ice (and falling through it on one occasion) ripping great right-angled tears in the bum of your breeks on the farmer's barbed wire fences and so on all called for some hasty improvisation with the darning or sewing needle before parents found out. Dungarees were a Godsend - and kept you warm too.

The gang warfare we boys had waged for years against the Macduffers prepared us well for the forthcoming hostilities against German paratroops. Binoculars had been placed strategically by the highest window in the Manse attic so that we could descry the very first falling parachutes of the Nazi hordes. Day by day at that time we awaited the tolling of the church bells which would be the signal that invasion by the enemy had begun. Needless to say, there were no church bells as normal on a Sunday before church. In our gang hut at the back of the Manse we had long planned what dire deeds of sabotage and mayhem our gang would wreak on the invaders.

The painfully ineffectual bumblings of a scantily armed Home Guard (originally the LDV or Local Defence Volunteers) had not convinced us that our fields and beaches where Churchill would have us fight to the last man were entirely safe in their hands. The "Look, Duck and Vanish" lads, as they were known, now "Dad's Army", consisted of the older schoolteachers, postmen and other men from "reserved occupations" or who were medically unfit for war service. We used to watch them drilling on Sundays as a light diversion from our study of aircraft identification manuals. They were not a patch on the Sandyhill Rifles.

In the light of what we saw, we little belligerents had therefore developed contingency plans for weeks beforehand which would enable us to wage a resistance war against any Nazis foolish enough to take on the Sandyhillers! In the Craw Widdie, a mile from the town, we had dug and lined with timber a dugout (hidden in deep undergrowth) where a secret cache of tinned food and water was buried along with some tools (for slackening the wheels of German

Army lorries etc.) lengths of wire (for garrotting and tripping) matches and paraffin (for fire raising) and some nasty looking Bowie knives and an old bayonet, well sharpened. We had even cemented an iron ring, bought with hard-earned pocket money from the local blacksmith, into the side of the high dyke by the main road just to the south of the town from which, hidden by bushes on the other side of the road, we could stretch a long piece of piano wire about head height across the road.

The given knowledge about the advance of German paratroops at that time was that they were dropped with folding bicycles which enabled them to make quick but silent progress into towns and villages they aimed to capture. We aimed to catch them as they advanced into Banff on their bikes from the open fields in the rural hinterland where we assumed they would be dropped. The idea was that the wire would be left slack, lying on the road, until the olive-green clad and jackbooted murderers were almost up to it, having accelerated down the nearby hill. We would then pull the wire taught with an iron bar for leverage fixed to the free end of it, to catch them at neck height. In the hoped for ensuing melee and slaughter we would make off at high speed through the woods and paths known only to ourselves. So ran the theory. The risk was that our mothers would call us in for tea just as the wretched Germans were approaching.

Nevertheless, the ring in the wall remains there to this day for all to see. Unfortunately, its rather low height in the wall not only represented our necessarily boyish limited working height, but also (because the wire would have been at bicyclist's neck height only on the left side of the road) our egocentric notion that invading Germans would comply with our traffic mores by riding on the left! "Links Fahren" notices might have helped.

Considering the great shortage of all kinds of both ferrous and non-ferrous metals at that time, it was a minor miracle that we could obtain these basic requirements for sabotage and resistance. But old Mr Conn the blacksmith had always been good for "a bittie o' hauf-roon" for runners for our sledges in the winter, and the odd request for something a bit different was gently indulged.

Just as everything seemed to pile up at great rate in historical time at the beginning of the war, so also did our boyish ploys have a sudden intensity which kept us out of sight of our parents for hours and hours at a time.

Certainly I have seen the intensity with which ten and eleven year old boys such as my eldest grandson can become absorbed in a topic like "spies", football, signalling systems and the like, so perhaps there is simply a developmental phase in a boy's life when boundless energies can be channeled into the current pursuit. In the case of our gang during the early '40's we turned all those energies, hounded and driven on by the propaganda of the time, into war oriented activities. It has never emerged whether we were unique in this respect. We kept our planning secret (in the manner of the time) but it is not unlikely that other lads about the town and district had similar pursuits and plans.

Looked at in retrospect, it is questionable whether, in the event of an invasion, we would have been able or allowed by our parents and the authorities to indulge any of the plans we had made, but at the time all was earnest endeavour. Most of us were already whipped up into a heady nationalism (British, not Scottish) both by events in the war, Churchill's rousing speeches, and the widespread campaign of propaganda from the Department of Psychological Warfare of the War Office, so it was hardly surprising that by 1943 or 1944 we could hardly wait to be called up, as our erstwhile schoolmates three years or so our senior already were, and to become fighter pilots or tank commanders.

In that psychological climate, what, in happier times would have been our normal play activities, became, in wartime, tinged with a kind of lawless aggression which converted the games we played into dress rehearsals for more serious combat. Most of us solemnly believed that we would either have to fight some sort of guerilla warfare if the Germans invaded, or we would in due course be called up into the regular Forces. In either event, it was our intention to be well prepared.

At the side of the Manse was a piece of rough ground, known to the family as "the quarry", which had so far resisted all my father's best efforts to effect any sort of cultivation. In the corner of this area stood the garden shed - a ten foot by ten foot tarred wooden shed which was the fighting HQ of our gang, "The Sandyhillers". To protect ourselves from the "Bartlett Placers" and the "Whinhillers" as much as from the Germans we dug a deep, and only partially shored dugout in the "quarry" and spent much of our free time arming it, like the one in the woods, with knives, catapults and approriately selected stones as ammunition.

We also attempted to heat it, with sometimes terrifying results, with a rickety wood-burning stove constructed from old tin boxes, a large inverted clay flower pot (for a flue) holding up an eight foot length of iron drainpipe to take the products of combustion up to the outer air. When it really got going the flames would roar loudly up the makeshift chimney, the latter would become nearly red hot and in due course we would have to abandon the dugout for fear of either blowing ourselves up (a moral victory for the Nazis which we could not contemplate) or cooking ourselves to a turn.

Although it was developed to accommodate a surfeit of rotten doo's (pigeon's) eggs acquired from one of our allies among the "Low Streeters", our *tour de force* of hideous weaponry was a gun which fired rotten eggs at enemy gang members. Much experimentation by myself, mainly, resulted in the barrel (another length of redundant iron pipe) being roped to a long wooden pole and propped on a wooden barrow or fallen tree trunk to achieve the necessary elevation and azimuth adjustments. The difficult bit was the construction of a breech and propellant force strong enough to fire the egg further than we could throw it without breaking it and releasing noxious amounts of hydrogen disulphide into the nearby air. Neither my mother nor the other gang members would have appreciated that one little bit.

There were some accidents with the prototype before we fixed up a cotton wool padded plunger of wood (a three foot length of old broom handle with a three inch diameter disc nailed to the distal end of it) driven, at the appropriate moment, up the pipe, egg and all, by the release of a two inch wide and three foot long strip of old lorry wheel inner tube lashed to a catapult-like "Y" frame level with the proximal end of the pipe. Eventually, finding the misfire rate with rotten eggs as high as the supply of these was erratic, we settled for ammunition in the form of stones. The greater flexibility of our own tried and trusted one-man catapults and the occasional airgun or home made crossbow resulted in the big gun's premature obsolescence.

Our fighting uniform was fairly standard for the time and greatly influenced by what we had been reading about Royal Marine Commando raids and other exploits. Navy blue dungarees, blue corduroy blouson or jersey, boots for rough work and plimsolls for night stealth attacks, and, of course, faces blackened by burnt cork and balaclavas covering most of our faces but for the eyes. Father's binoculars were handy and codes and secret signals were many and varied - and sometimes agreed on. In this guise, our gang of trainee saboteurs and renegades got up to tricks and exploits which would, in this day and age, be roundly condemned by all and sundry. Boys being caught nowadays engaging in activities such as we undertook during the war would almost certainly finish up before the Children's Panel or worse.

Naturally, the commissariat had to be enhanced in summer and autumn by occasional raids on, preferably, since the challenge was greater, the Chief Constable's apples and plums and a few neeps and carrots from the fields. There was a story prevalent among us that it was not illegal to take one turnip or one carrot from a field of growing crops so long as it was eaten there and then and no more were taken. There are similar laws in some other Mediterranean countries but we never put the matter to test by doing our best to be discreet when the "bobby" was about.

The wars between our gangs were sporadic affairs of varying severity. There was a constant search for "secret weapons" like our rotten egg gun and to combat this, espionage and spying reconnaissances were staged, usually under cover of the long and deep darkness of the blackout. These commando raids involved gang members penetrating the streets, gardens, and sometimes even houses of our "enemy" gangsters in order to overhear vital conversations in which plotting and sedition directed against the "Sandyhillers" might feature. These ventures became ever more daring and risky as, whipped on by the challenges of our pals, we would be challenged to crawl about the backyards and gardens of our neighbours and report back to the "gang hut" what activities, and, better still, what conversations we had spied.

This exercise went a long way toward confirming to me too early in life the utterly mundane and boring nature of day-to-day life in a small town. Occasionally, there were eye-openers which made our hours in the mud, leaves, and sometimes snow, all worthwhile. Then came the decision as to how much to tell. Some of our gang members were less trustworthy than others - and some were not of sufficiently mature years, as we would cruelly remind them, for their ears to be assailed by the whole salacious or simply curious detail thus observed. In retrospect, we were fairly loathsome little rascals then - and we were never caught. The Nazis were very lucky not to have invaded Banff!

It is possible that our having lived in a small town, relatively cut off from the wider world, or indeed the rest of Britain, made our indulgence in activities of such wildness possible in a way which would neither have been tolerated by the adult world nor seemed appropriate to our urban peers. We were all in a kind of time capsule. There was no such thing as television and very little radio. Written communication with our age peers in the cities was negligible and the general level of censorship in the newspapers meant that we had no external standards against which to evaluate how we behaved. William Golding's "Lord of the Flies" had not been published until the '50's, so our early pubertal and pre-pubertal fantasies were nourished on the likes of R L Stevenson's "Treasure Island", R M Ballantine's "Coral Island", Captain W E Johns' "Biggles" exploits, the adventures of Dixon Hawke and various outrageous boyish dramas in the pages of the "Wizard" or "Hotspur" comics.

Perhaps more than any of these, the pages of the daily newspapers with their stories of military derring do and their dramatic pictures from war correspondents and photographers, were what drove our imaginations and thus our "play". We would, of course, have been grievously insulted had our behaviour been thus described. After all, do not the psychologists tell us that the so-called play of the young of many species is but a preparation for the survival activities and serious conflicts and other vital behaviours in adult life?

Not all aspects of our young lives were taken up in these days by school, football and gang warfare, however. The enforced absence of fathers, big brothers and sisters and even uncles and cousins, left mothers with heavy burdens so far as managing and controlling their rowdier offspring was concerned. Most of us, though my brother and I were exceptions, lived in a female dominated world, except in secondary school, and during the all too brief occasions when the men came home on leave.

This led, often without due recognition being paid to them, to the important social and educational role fulfilled by those devoted members of the public (again often women) in towns large and small throughout the country who devoted substantial chunks of their free time to running youth organisations like the Boy Scouts, the Girl Guides and the Boys' Brigade. At least one night of the week, year in and year out, many of us were organised with varying degrees of vigour and competence, in a way which enlarged our understanding of hobbies, social and personal obligations and sports too. And all this often in the face of privations such as meeting in a hall, dimly lit because of the blackout and the need to save energy, unheated and with few disposable resources, and often at times when they might have had many better things to do.

In the summer months at least we could engage in outdoor pursuits less clandestine than we might otherwise have undertaken and there was always the chance that some of the more senior and/or responsible seeming

The author and his young brother, Tom, in the Boys' Brigade during the early war years.

lads might go to camp in the holidays. But even that was difficult to the point of near impossibility because of Police regulations and the fact that tents tended to signify the military and we might be attacked by enemy raiders if we were spotted. Later in the war we were eventually allowed limited camping at first in the near vicinity of a town, and later, if no more than two bell tents (of virtually unmanageably hard and unresilient canvas) might be pitched briefly if suitably camouflaged with brown and green paint and hidden away among the secret fastnesses of, say, Dufftown or the Cabrach. German agents or reconnaisance planes were not thought to be likely to examine such areas in detail. Even the then Banffshire County Council sometimes seemed to jib at that!

Easily the most memorable camp was one in a July near the end of the war, when, due to some wonderful adminisrative oversight, a group of Scouts and BB's found themselves pitched in a field in upper Banffshire adjacent to one occupied by a troop (if that's the correct collective noun) of Girl Guides. Truly it was said that "The boy scouts and the girl guides!", but when the powers that be actually saw the risk of this aphorism being put to the test in all too realistic a way, there were hurried conferences and camp was struck in what we thought was unwarrantably quick time and we enthusiastic males were "flitted", lock, stock and barrel, ten miles or so away to where we could not "loosen the girls' guyropes" or otherwise indulge our camp craft. In the 1940's "camping around" meant something completely different from what it does now!

What we did learn was to live off the land economically and without damage to the environment in any way; to snare rabbits for the pot, catch the odd trout (and a few illegally taken salmon parr) in the burns and boil in our dixie tins tatties scrounged from friendly farmers. Seven or eight years later, these self-same skills became relevant and necessary when I was subjected to the rigours of what were laughingly described as "escape and evasion" exercises in the RAF.

That apart, my years in the Lifeboys and the BB's did, through the efforts and dedication of those adults committed enough to lead us, endow me with a lifelong interest and, I hope, understanding of the natural history around us, a preparedness to get along with kids of varying backgrounds and abilities, a habit of cooperation but a spirit of competitiveness where it was appropriate and a readiness to make our own entertainment. Children and teenagers of today will perhaps find it hard to grasp that then we had few households with a radio, no such thing as television, only a lucky few had bicycles and the cinema was, at best, a once a week adventure to watch Movietone News and a black and white movie starring William Boyd as Hopalong Cassidy (always a goodie), or a very young John Mills gritting his (very regular and white) teeth as he struggled to bring home a convoy of supply ships across a stormy Atlantic seething with U-boats. Real luxury was a Saturday night at the Picture House (9 old pence), a bag of chips and a "Green Final". If Deveronvale had won, so much the better!

School imposed what I now recognise as a useful routine on our days. Those of us whose Dads were "away in the war" were not given too much time to brood on the dire possibilities that entailed. I cannot remember any of my pals believing anything other than that their Dads would return at the end of it all - the "It'll never happen to me!" syndrome usefully at work. Perhaps the fact that we were at all times surrounded by soldiers of our own and other Allied countries gave a sort of immediacy to our experience of armies, and the absence of too much shooting was reassuring. After all, most of my kind were only filling in time at school until we ourselves could join the Forces and kill a few Germans or Japs. It was made hard for us to think of them as people like ourselves living out their lives with complementary attitudes, though I doubt whether many little Hansies in the Schwartzwald ever considered whether they might be invaded and have to plan their defences as we did in the Craw Widdie.

CHAPTER 9

VISITATIONS

Ever since Dunkirk, our house had an almost permanent complement of Servicemen and women. Sometimes they stayed for a while in some of the spare rooms, sometimes they visited the dining room (which was, to our eyes, quite posh) in a mood of high good humour tinged with both anxiety and wistfulness. This was the room my father used for weddings and sometimes baptisms. Church of Scotland Parish ministers have always taken a liberal view of ceremonial if not of the vows taken in the course of it, and many a young soldier, sailor or airman tied the knot right there in the course of a snatched 48-hour pass, or a few days' leave between convoys or battles somewhere on the face of the war-torn earth.

The fact that there were so many comings and goings at the Manse may in itself have made it a convenient "safe house" for certain other purposes. Most of the Service personnel who were put up for the night were simply those we had come to know well because they came from far flung parts of the country and could not take advantage of short leaves of 48 hours or so because of the sheer difficulty of getting home and back in that time. One of these, Bert Brooks-Effard was a Channel Islander in the RAF who continued to send a Christmas card to us, even after my parents' deaths and indeed up to the time of his own death not many years ago. His home islands were, of course, then occupied by the Germans and he knew little of the fate of his family there. I remember him as a distinguished looking, greying man with an effortless politeness and charm but who seemed to like us boys as well as our parents and who brought some of his RAF pals with him to play whist of an evening or just have a chat and a beer in the parlour.

We even played temporary hosts to oddly important personnel who often turned up of an evening in uniform, sometimes Army, sometimes Naval, but who, after a day or two and perhaps a night as well, would leave in strangely assorted civilian clothes - a fisherman's jersey and seaboots over a boilersuit, or an ill fitting serge suit, with a bonnet and small case. The fact that they seemed to head either for the harbour at Macduff or Buckie when they left us suggested, to me at least, that they might have been agents (the acceptible name for spies) on their way to Norway or Denmark. They were all bi- or tri-lingual and several have left their autographs (with little or no embellishment other than their names, Norwegian or British, on the page.) We never saw them again although the officers who had spent many hours with them during their stay in Banff did appear at our dinner table from time to time afterwards. It is probable that some never returned.

The Nissen huts around Duff House and the House itself, after its short life as a POW Camp, became a military base for a polyglot variety of Army regiments. We played host to Poles, with some Ukrainians among them; to Free French, in small numbers; to many (mostly Scottish) Regiments, the HLI, the Cameronians and the Argyll and Sutherland Highlanders, and the KOSBies, as they were known - the King's Own Scottish Borderers. Their impact on the town varied.

Most liked of all were the 42nd Norwegian Mountain Brigade, many of whom had escaped from their own occupied country by very hazardous small boat voyages across the stormy, cold, dark and wintry North Sea. They were led by King Haakon VII and Kronprinz Olav, later to become King of Norway. During the snows of winter these soldiers would both amaze and entertain us by their prowess on skis. Many were capable, and some did, of ski jumping over the railway halfway up the Hill o'Doune when the snow was deep enough. We were later to learn, of course, that some of them were mountain men who were also accomplished ski jumpers, racers and instructors and who, in happier times, would have been the glamour boys of the piste and the moguls in the eyes of the young folk who would have been their pupils. Now they marched and sang, trained and sang, skied and sang and eventually married our girls and sang. These almost always turned out to be stable marriages and several such couples are still alive and well, living all over Norway, to this day.

The Norwegians were largely Lutheran and my father was

also their officiating Chaplain. He eventually worked in double harness, so to speak, with a Pastor Dahle, and began, as it was his wont always to try to get to grips with some new language, to learn Norwegian with his help. Pastor Dahle was a relaxed and pleasant man. The most outstanding memory I have of him, however, was of the immaculately pleated ruff he wore over his gown when he was in the pulpit - the equivalent of my father's "bands", two tabs of linen worn below his clerical collar on ceremonial occasions. My father and he would retreat into the study of an afternoon from where they would emerge well after I had returned from school.

My parents had always held "open house" to all ranks of the Services who wanted, once in a while, to enjoy simple home comforts of an evening or weekend. In consequence, Tom and I would meet and talk with all manner of soldiers, sailors and airmen of all ranks and many with experiences such as we had only read of in books. Some may have been tempted to "shoot a line" or two, but many told unembellished tales that had our eyes on stalks and our ears twitching. All shared the comfort of the parlour for a bite of tea and a sing-song or a game of cards. How my mother managed this on our meagre rations I'll never know. My guess is that she was helped out by her friends and others who knew of the work she was doing for these young men and women.

When very senior officers happened to arrive, however, my mother's sense of the proprieties forced her to put on the fire in the drawing room upstairs. Up there were the piano, the display cabinets with her "wedding china" and strange little items from the Orient (or Birmingham) left by the many missionaries who had been our pre-war guests, the aspidistra, a few half-decent watercolours and prints (two Farquharsons and a Whistler were amongst those I remember best) and some Persian rugs. The card table and cards there were less dog-eared and greasy with use than those downstairs and everybody at the table had a pencil and score card (of Utility paper!).

One night I had occasion to try and draw my father's attention to help me with some homework. He was at the time in the drawing room and I was in the process of figuring out some stratagem whereby I could winkle him out from the bridge game which had followed dinner. Suddenly the door opened and a tall and distinguished military gentleman emerged (to head, I think, for the bathroom). His chest bespattered with medals and resplendent with gold cord on his epaulets, he was, to me, as like Sir C Aubrey Smith, the actor in such films as "The Prisoner of Zenda" or "The Mark of Zorro" as I was likely to see in the flesh. In fact, he turned out to be a General Strugstad, ADC to Kronprinz Olav of Norway, taken along by Prinz Olav to make up a four for bridge with my parents. My mother was a bit of a bridge addict, but, as I found out later, much given to assertive post-mortems after every hand. Naturally, it was always her partner or her opponent who had wrongly led the two of clubs or failed to finesse in the third trick. In spite of this, the Prinz seemed to enjoy his visits and both he and the General would try me on a few words of Norwegian, or even more in French, in which the General at least was fluent.

There was also one occasion when King Haakon VII himself paid us a brief visit. He was billeted in the Fife Arms Hotel in the town for the short time he spent, mostly inspecting his troops and no doubt boosting their morale considerably. We knew then, and have much later strongly confirmed, that the Norwegians have a very sincere regard for their flag and for their Royal Family - a family which, in its turn, showed its every member to be fundamentally democratic, of the people in every sense, approachable and, above all modest about their authority and responsibilities. When the king and crown prince spoke to me from time to time in the Manse, it was almost as if they gave you the impression they were honoured by the conversation and not *vice versa.* They certainly seemed to me to embody some of the finest of Scandinavian traits of openness and honesty and although we knew that they had armed Norwegian soldiers in their truck outside our front door (and, for all I knew, elsewhere around the house) while they were with us, they were relaxed and genial with my parents and clearly enjoyed the dinner, cards and chatter of a domestic environment. In these dark days for them, or indeed for all of us, it must have seemed like a little oasis of calm and normality.

Of course these were but the high spots of the daily round. My father had very much more to do with the ordinary Norwegian soldiers who needed his pastoral care. The roles now assumed by psychologists and counsellors were then fulfilled almost exclusively by ministers, solicitors and general medical practitioners. These men, many of whom had escaped from their homeland amid imminent danger of death and the hazards and privations of secret voyages across the sea in sometimes tiny boats had deep anxieties about their families, their own peace of mind and the future which my father would do his best to alleviate in one way or another. And, happily, as well as counselling them as best he could, he married quite a few of them in the church or in the dining room, just as they chose, to local girls, and just occasionally to Norwegian girls who had escaped the occupation in some other way.

At the end of the war, and, I think in recognition of all that both my parents had done for the Norwegians of all ranks in our midst, a silver plaque was placed in St Mary's Parish Church of Banff, and my father personally was awarded the Freedom Medal of Norway. He was extremely proud of that, perhaps as much as he later was of his Doctorate in Divinity from the University of Edinburgh.

Although military visitors predominated during the earlier years of the war, and were present by invitation rather than, as our evacuees and rescued soldiers from Dunkirk were, by diktat, there were a number of disparate visitors also. Only some of the names in my mother's autograph book have reminded me of these for they were essentially transients, with us for an hour or two, or one night at most. Prior to that, many of the soldiers and airmen and women who were with us repeatedly had become almost like members of the family and they moved with an easy familiarity between the parlour and the kitchen, helping with the dishes, fetching coal for the fire or having a kick at a ball with us out in the back garden.

The "transients" certainly included the possible "spies" I have speculated about earlier. They also included visiting professional entertainers, broadcasters and producers and actors and actresses from the BBC or ENSA. Alongside names like those of actresses Ann Todd and Dame Sybil Thorndike are those of Elizabeth Adair, later to become a prominent BBC producer and writer, and, no doubt in the town in some other context entirely, Lady Aberdeen, Lord Rowallan and the Moderator of the Church of Scotland, then the

VISITATIONS

Very Reverend Dr James Black - a very jolly man as I remember, and one of the few visitors who could make a major social occasion out of a very simple breakfast.

Perhaps one of the pleasantest things about visitors, and the signatories of my mother's wee book during the war, was that alongside and intermingled with the names of the "Great and the Good" were the names, wishes and comments of many ordinary, day-by-day friends of the family, relatives, neighbours, schoolteachers and the like.

These included the signature of my favourite Primary school teacher, a Mrs Kelly. In those days there were almost no "Mrs" among lady teachers because of the then view among County Education Committees that only single ladies were proper for the education of the young. Perhaps married ladies might corrupt the youth of the city by knowing too much about sex and things like that. Mrs Kelly was in fact a widow, and so far as I knew, childless. Nevertheless, she was unlike all the other teachers I had ever had in that she simply seemed to have not only an understanding, but a willingness to understand, a child's mind allied to a capacity to make all sorts of things about the world interesting to us. I owe her much.

Other children at that time probably had visitors in their houses too. The town, after all, had played host to a succession of soldiers of several lands who were not confined to barracks all the time. At one time too there were just under 500 child evacuees (although only about 180 remained for any length of time) at first. Many of their relatives would visit for a weekend or a day from time to time, though in the end only a handful of the children stayed long enough to become aculturalised to the Northeast. Strangely, we seemed not to talk to each other much about what went on in our houses. For many, it might have seemed either to tempt fate, or simply to be imprudent, to invite in to their homes strangers when fathers and brothers were away fighting. For others, the stringencies of rationing may have been more difficult to bypass.

While the soldiers had been in their Nissen huts round Duff House and elsewhere, however, bulldozers and scrapers had been busy only a mile or two to the west. Lorry loads of shingle and sand had rumbled through the town, night and day for weeks, and eventually a great new aerodrome was hewn from the fields and moorland beyond Boyndie and the town became a billet for a brand new batch of combatants and their families. Most of the former, Norwegian, Commonwealth and British, were necessarily based on the 'drome itself, but the young wives and sweethearts and some children came to find digs and rented rooms in the town while the Banff Strike Wing was formed and became operational at RAF Banff.

CHAPTER 10

MAX AND THE MOSQUITOS

As the war drew on, I was aware of my attitudes subtly changing as I moved up the school. Banff had not, after all suffered the Blitzkrieg of Rotterdam or Warsaw. The immediate threat of invasion gradually receded as the Nazis were repulsed from the heart of Russia and the 8th Army marched westward along the North African coast. Alamein, Tobruk and then Bizerta and Tunis fell to Alexander and Montgomery. Even Rommel, held in some awe by ourselves, perhaps more than, for example, Generals Jodl or Keitel, was found to be beatable. The U-boats had been defeated, largely by airborne radar, in the Atlantic and massive bombing raids were being inflicted on the Ruhr and on the heart of the German Fatherland, even Berlin. There was a feeling that the tide of war had turned fundamentally our way.

Another reason for this burgeoning optimism was that in Banff itself, at least since the middle of 1942, there had been a sense of involvement, not with apprehensive defence against invasion and possible defeat, but with offence and victory. This had grown with every lorry load of shingle that had been laboriously dug up by American supplied Caterpillar scrapers and bulldozers (even the name was new to us then) on the shore of the Palmer Cove and driven by straining diesels up to the new airfield at Boyndie, just to the west of the town. With incredible effort and expertise, this airfield was started and finished, all the incidental buildings and defences complete, in little over a year.

The shoreline never recovered, but soon the spring sunshine of 1943 shone on the bright yellow livery of a host of Oxford twin-engined training aircraft, together with a few Ansons, used to give advanced pilot training on twin-engined aircraft. The airfield was seldom quiet while the weather allowed and although the early marques of the Oxford had some vices (and I spent many hours in them myself flying all around the south of England and southwest approaches in the RAF almost nine years later) the safety and output record of Banff in terms of trained pilots was very good. Official records indicate that over 1500 fully trained pilots emerged in the course of the year before the Strike Wing of Beaufighters and Mosquitos took over the 'drome.

Then the rather pedestrian radial engines of the Oxfords gave way to the resonant throb of the Rolls Royce "Merlin" engines of the Mosquitos and the "whispering death" of the quieter Beaufighters. RAF Banff became a Wing strength (i.e. from three to as many as six squadrons) Strike Force of Beaufighter and Mosquito fighter/bombers. The aircrew were mainly Norwegian, from the Commonwealth and British and many were billeted locally with their families. All the squadrons were under the command of Group Captain Max Aitken, ex-Battle of Britain pilot and son of the late Lord Beaverbrook, the newspaper magnate who had been at one period of the war Minister for Aircraft Production.

Although the summer weather in this part of North Scotland can be pleasantly dry and sunny, much of the operational time crews spent while at RAF Banff was through the winters of 1943/4 and 1944/5. To many, it must have been a bleak experience. Not only was the 280 foot high plateau on which the airfield sat swept by cruelly biting winds, often with more north than west in them, but it

A view of Banff in 1945 as lines of Mosquitos assemble on the perimeter track heading for the runway to take off on another attack on shipping in the Norwegian fjords.   (via Chaz Bowyer)

could be even more featureless when snowbound or swathed in the driving drizzle and Scotch mist of autumn and spring. Much of the maintenance work and arming of the aircraft was done out on dispersal pads where there was no shelter from the hostile elements and the ominous sough of the wind in the surrounding trees must have made a bleak accompaniment to the patter of the rain on the aircraft. The fact that the Strike Wing was subject to a casualty rate much higher proportionately than any other in the RAF at the time made it no easier to bear. Needless to say, it failed to stop us boys from cycling out several times a week to watch everything from the testing of the cannon at the range on the northeast side of the aerodrome to the arrival after action of the war-torn aircraft.

For those who have a technical interest in the functioning of RAF Banff during those times there is a wealth of detail to be found in two books, one by Jim Hughes, "A Steep Turn to the Stars" and the other by David J Smith, "Action Stations: No 7". Both of these writers have pointed out that, unlike other combat units of the RAF, the Strike Wings at Banff and Dallachy to the west were involved the more as the Axis war machine retreated from Europe toward Norway, where it was once thought Hitler's forces would organise themselves for a last stand. Shipping in the form of "flak" ships, transports, cargo vessels and U-boats therefore congregated in the sea area around Denmark and Norway, especially in and on the approaches to the western fjords. There was even rather more German fighter activity there in the latter months of the war than anywhere and vicious dogfights between the Mosquitos from Banff and supporting Mustangs from Peterhead against Focke Wulf 190's and Messerschmidt 109's and 110's often resulted from the former's attacks in the fjords.

In that setting, not only did the aircrews fatigue and need the occasional morale booster but so did the ground crews also. Stressed not only by the hectic action arming and preparing in a thousand other ways the planes before an operation, but almost as much by waiting for their charges and friends to return, they would welcome some relaxation off the base. Many local people did their best to see that this was made available in a whole variety of ways although many of the personnel became so tired that even the business of organising transport to visit the neighbouring towns could make too many emotional demands on them.

Just as dozens of the ground crews and WAAFs from the radio sites, cookhouses and ammunition dumps had over the months visited the Manse for a relaxed evening of cards, a sing-song or just a quiet chat, so also did a number of the senior officers become friendly with my parents and brother Tom and myself. It lent a certain cachet when we were able to tell the lads at school that Max Aitken (his own personal aircraft, a "Mosquito", had red painted spinners) had taken us in it at the weekend as well as showing us the Ops. Room, gunnery ranges, air traffic control room and tower and other mysteries. It was little wonder that "633 Squadron" was later to become one of my favourite films. The blyth insouciance which I remember being associated with my entry to the Station Commander's office at Banff in 1944 contrasted markedly with later visits to "The Groupie's" office I had occasion to make in the early 1950's when I was a very junior Pilot Officer.

Sir Max, as he was later to become, thoroughly enjoyed my father's sense of the ridiculous, his cavalier approach (unlike my mother's) to bridge and his liberal views on religion. When he was not on ops. himself, he would often drop in, sometimes with a rather mad Northern Irish full-time RAF padre from the base (whose stunning looking wife I was prematurely, though privately, besotted with) and play cards till the early hours of the morning. After the war he arranged for my father to be taken down, at his expense, to London, where he baptised Sir Max's children.

RAF Banff quickly became a very busy, and seriously operational, base for strikes against German and Axis shipping and installations in and around the Norwegian fjords. Although there were some night operations, the usual pattern of events was for the squadrons, heavily loaded with explosive rockets, cannon shells and bombs, to take off around midday and, orbiting the town and environs, sort themselves out into their combat formations before diving to just over sea level and heading east past Troup Head for Norway.

For young lads like us, these morning operations held nothing like the gut-wrenching tension, apprehension and danger they must have held for the aircrews taking part in them. The early morning briefings about the day's operation, weather conditions all the way across the grey and often stormy North Sea to the looming walls of the Norwegian fjords, the opposition they might be expected to face (and it was frequently extremely fierce) and the logistics of bomb load, fuel levels and navigation, must have been sober and testing minutes for each and every two-man crew. Several would not return.

We saw only the glamour and the adventure, however. The busy cacophony of engine noise as the planes took off in sequence and formated over and around the town was guaranteed to disturb our attempted concentration on our lessons, or better still, if it happened during the dinner hour (as it often did) football or chatter

Aircraft of Banff Strike Wing attacking shipping in Norwegian waters.

was suspended as we critically watched the flights organise themselves. Then, no doubt on a pre-arranged signal, the aircraft, in characteristic "V" formations, would head off to the east or east-north-east and dive low to perhaps a couple of hundred feet over the malevolent grasping fingers of the cold wavetops. They had to find Sogne or Hardanger Fjords, or some subtly hidden arms of these, and do their damage before the enemy coastal radar picked them up.

In retrospect, there was a gruesome harshness which I am

sure none of us recognised at the time, in the way we then settled to
our problems in trigonometry, English literature or abstruse Latin
constructions. We pored over our books and quailed before the
wrath of our teachers during these very hours when men little more
than four or five years our senior fought for their lives (and ours)

The Operations Room at RAF Banff which the author visited, as a boy, with Group
Captain Max Aitken, the Station Commander.

amid a hail of "flak" and tracer shells. Each one of these brave and
often frightened men was equally trying in his way to deal out death
and destruction to the enemy. There was, of course, nothing new
about that. It had been happening every day and night of the war for
years elsewhere. What gave it immediacy for us then was the fact
that we had come to know the actual personalities involved - the
men, their wives and girl friends, and to sense the real tension and
stress for all of them, day in, day out, as the conflict went on. When
we watched the planes returning and anxiously compared the count
in with the count out, saw the damaged and burning, half-wrecked
airframes being coaxed in over the sea and then the airfield,
wondered whether some had ditched or crash-landed at a satellite

100field like Fraserburgh or Dallachy, the war somehow touched us more closely.

In the High Street and back gardens, the wives would count them out - and, three or four hours later, anxiously count them in again. Sogne, Stavanger and Hardanger Fjords were their frequent destinations; all highly predictable by the German defenders and all strongly protected by fixed guns and "flak" ships. The targets were made all the more difficult often by lying deep between steep mountains, forcing the attacking aircraft to run in along the fjords, often very low.

In simple flying terms, the margins of safety were very low. With the concomitant problems of avoiding the anti-aircraft fire and still pressing successful attacks on the shipping or other installations they became negligible. Not least of the difficulties was the fact that often attacks on ground targets or shipping could only be made by one or perhaps two aircraft at a time, so narrow was the airspace available. Other aircraft had to hang about in the vicinity and then come in in their turn. In consequence the enemy gunners not only could predict the line of attack with great certainty, they could also concentrate all their fire on just the one or two planes attacking. Those waiting their turn to join in the attack also became vulnerable to fighter attack and had no advantage of height with which to meet it.

It is not surprising therefore that these crews were subject to a high casualty rate and very high personal stress levels. There was no question of stress counselling or stress management in those days. They just had to come home, have a few beers or a pie and beans in the NAAFI and get on with it next day....and the next.....and the next - if they survived.

The wear and tear was bound to show, both at home and in the local pubs but both wives and townsfolk knew what was going on and were remarkably tolerant. My father's pastoral skills were mainly required by the families more than by the flyers and the Norwegians who comprised a significant number of the worst hit squadron were often escapees from their own country early in the war whose contacts with home were negligible and whose burning hatred of the Nazis drove them to truly awesome limits of endurance, courage and sometimes foolhardiness. Because of their local knowledge of the coastline and of the convoluted topography of the fjords, these Norwegian pilots and navigators, mostly members of 333 squadron, I think, were often used to reconnoitre and lead the attacks.

If casualties were quite high, there were also some notable victories too. The latter were marked by a variety of high jinks in and around the town, reinforced by alcohol. One night, in the spring of 1945, I think, we were wakened from our sleep by the church bell sounding in a markedly erratic fashion. The first assumption was that we had, after all, been invaded by the Germans. We had not. We had been invaded by a band of drunken aircrews from the 'drome who had just returned from a highly successful and totally victorious night operation and who had decided that the town should know and that the ringing of the church bell was the sure way to inform them.

In due course, the beadle, the police and the Military Police intervened to put paid to the one-note carillon. They also put the damper on (if that is not a ludicrously inept metaphor in this instance) some casual swimming in the huge Emergency Water Supply tank which had sat with its wire mesh covering undisturbed for three years or so at the foot of Institution Terrace. Throughout all these celebrations there was a notable lack of choral restraint even when the Whitecaps appeared but this tended to die down as first, the bell ringers, then the swimmers and finally a simple bunch of post-graduate-standard drinkers was winkled out of the "Royal Oak".

The story went, and I have never been able to authenticate this, that a fairly strong force of our Mosquitos had set out on a night raid heading for somewhere like the south of Norway or north Denmark when our own fighter controllers picked up on long range radar a force of slower and heavier German torpedo bombers heading west not long after their take-off. Whether the Mosquitos' original raid was abandoned in favour of this "juicy" target or not, it seems that the Banff Mosquitos were able to hit the enemy aircraft at a time when they were off guard because they were then so far from the UK coast. As a result the German force suffered massive losses against only negligible losses of our own aircraft. Coming as it did after a period when the Banff Wing had suffered losses itself, such a triumph deserved a bit of a "blow-out", even if it was nearly three in the morning!

With our aspirations to join them as soon as our age and the continuation of the war allowed, several of us lads would, after school, ride our bikes out to the edge of the airfield at Whyntie farm, on the northern edge of the airfield, to see in the returning planes. Sometimes all went well and we would count in the aircraft, damaged and intact alike. There was always a good deal of agreement as to how many had gone out. There were just too many observers for a general average of the counts to be too far wrong. What we often failed to recognise was that some of the aircraft returning might have taken off from other airfields, and similarly,

some which did not appear again might have landed elsewhere.

Sometimes, however, we felt as if some of the battered and smoking (and sometimes flaming) aircraft and their two-man crews would land on our heads as we crouched against the dyke. Planes would come in on one engine, the other pouring smoke and often with parts of the wings, tail and control surfaces shot away. In they swept, yawing and dipping, one after the other, occasionally making spark-showered belly landings while the ambulance and fire tender raced after them.

One late afternoon, when the aircraft had come in widely scattered, usually a bad sign, and many badly damaged, I watched a Mosquito pilot, so low that I could clearly see that the cockpit canopy had been largely shot away and that the observer/bomb aimer was slumped, perhaps wounded or dead, in the right hand seat. To my horror, either one of his rockets or a bomb had "hung up". It had not released and could not be jettisoned and, worse still, one of his undercarriage legs seemed to be waggling about, unlocked down and not rigid at all. As he touched down it collapsed and I watched the aircraft skid and slide sideways along the runway, licks of flame appearing under it as it careered off the concrete on to the grass. Just as I thought the soft grass might prevent the bomb going off, there was a huge explosion and when the smoke and flame died down, not much of the plane was left. It seemed to have hit a building. The story went around, nevertheless, that that crew, incredibly, actually survived the crash.

It was possible that the pilot, who could have baled out over the sea close to the shore, had tried to land the plane for the sake of his wounded observer. It was not surprising that many of the aircrew were decorated for outstanding bravery on these hazardous operations. We knew all about them, but they were not given much publicity in the national press at the time. Perhaps there were special reasons for that but it seemed unfair when the bomber and fighter crews in the south and over Germany and the rest of Europe were still getting a good press coverage within the limits of censorship. At the time, my curiosity and interest in military planes and operations perhaps prevented a strong emotional reaction to that event. I can remember being rather quiet and thoughtful riding back home, but the greater and more immediate anxiety occasioned by having to get a Latin version perfect for the morrow took over after teatime.

Perhaps too, we were becoming inured to tragedy and death after four years of war. On a number of occasions aircraft crashed into fields near the aerodrome soon after take off because of pilot error or an engine or airframe failure. These, because of the relatively large load of bombs, rockets and fuel involved, were invariably fatal. Some of the crews were inevitably fresh from flying school and operational conversion units and the stress of multiple take offs in limited time coupled with restrictions on the available airspace and limitations on the aircraft's performance because of loadings, weather and visibility could impose pressures in excess of their capacity to cope. Sometimes too the sheer compression of a large number of aircraft manoeuvering at relatively low altitude while very heavily loaded made things very difficult for the pilots. Often Beaufighters from Dallachy would join up with Mosquitos from Banff while more aircraft were still taking off from the aerodrome. One such episode led to two Beaufighters crashing near Ordens farm only a mile or so from the airfield after colliding in midair. Four good crew died tragically and suddenly.

Other crashes occurred when the crews were practising rocket firing on the range near Tarlair, just outside the town of Macduff, a mile or two to the east of the airfield. These rockets were powerful weapons which had significantly boosted the firepower of the Beaufighter and Mosquito although they added significantly to the weight on the wings. Eight were normally slung under the wings, four on each side, and came to be used with considerable success against both enemy shipping and elsewhere against tanks and railway trains, bridges and so on in the preliminaries to and in the course of the campaign in Europe after D-day. It has been said that these rockets, together with their cannon and machine guns, gave Mosquitos the fire power of a naval cruiser - a forbidding thought to anyone being strafed by them.

Sometimes, unfortunately, these weapons, having been ignited, "hung up" and did not fall free of the aircraft as intended. The rocket force intended to drive them with increasing speed toward their targets was added to the thrust of the aircraft's engines and the plane might be unable to pull out of the diving attack in time, especially if it happened at low level, as was often the case in attacks against shipping or ground targets. One such event led to the crash of a Mosquito near an outdoor swimming pool (not in use because of the war, and the season) at Macduff when we were watching it practise at a target anchored in the sea near the shore. Because the Mosquito was largely constructed of balsa wood (just like we made model planes with at home) it would totally disintegrate on hitting the ground in such a crash. Only the engines and perhaps some of the guns and instruments would be recognisable. The crew had no chance to bail out at such low levels and high speeds.

However, off we cycled to see whether we could salvage

some cannon shells or perhaps a compass or radio set. As it happened, and perhaps it was just as well, the Macduff police and an RAF rescue team had arrived there first and it was days before we could pick about among the little wreckage left. The RAF rescue squad had tidied everything recognisable or usable away and the tide had swept away much of the balsa wood. Two more families were left to grieve.

The rapid construction and development, intense combat activity level and the sheer impact of warlike realities which the aerodrome brought into our lives was something which many of the townspeople and youths like myself treated with a kind of awe. True, we felt empowered and confident, even proud, when we saw the potential for destruction which took off, circled and departed many days of every week for many months.

Adults had more empathy with the families of those airmen who risked so much every day than had we young lads. All we wanted was to grow older quickly enough to be able to join them and fly these magnificent machines. School was a way of filling in the intervening period while we grew up. But after a bad day when several failed to return and when some children suddenly left school to drift away to mourn elsewhere, there would be times when we felt the stab of guilt, the wounds of war which go unseen, and our youthful resolution might weaken. But we never mentioned that to our pals. My father and his faithful parishioners prayed for those who died on this side of the ocean. We all grieved for all of them whether they returned or not. But it was in the nature of things that for many who failed to return, there were no funerals.

CHAPTER 11

FINALE

Then, in the early summer of 1944, with the change in emphasis of the way the war was going, there seemed to be troop movements such as we had never seen, even at the beginning of the war or at the time of Dunkirk. Every other day, long convoys of troop lorries, field guns, Bren gun carriers and tanks would rumble through or into the town or would deploy themselves in the fields and woods around the town while housewives plied all and sundry with tea and sandwiches scrimped from their own meager rations. Naturally, everybody sensed that "something big" was afoot.

By this time too, our dugouts in the Craw Widdie had been raided by ourselves. The rusting tins of beans and the "secret weapons" of sabotage and childish mayhem were used on other ploys. Now the sights of the older boys in school were firmly set on being Spitfire pilots, tank commanders or submariners - even moreso now that we thought we were winning than when things were pretty black. I was no exception and when boys from further up the school "escaped" to serve King and Country, and, worse still, could actually be seen by all of us flaunting their new found powers either when they appeared on post-training leave, resplendent in new uniforms, or in the air above us, circling the town in a Mustang or Spitfire, our impatience to be with them knew no bounds. Sandy Gordon and at least one other, by now in the RAF, "shot up" the school or the town centre in such planes and we were all mightily impressed when Neil Paterson visited the school on leave from the ship or submarine on which he was by then a Lieutenant. After the war he was to go on to become an acclaimed novelist and film script writer, the writer of "The China Run" and "Behold Thy Daughter". In the "pegs" (where we hung our coats) at school there was a good deal of talk as to whether the war would last long enough for us to be called up and "show off" similarly.

Typical of boys, we could not disguise our ambivalence about our Service seniors. On the one hand, each of us was bound to describe them to our pals as "bloody show-offs", while secretly feeling slightly jealous and not a little proud of them too. But at last the tide of war was really turning. The "Second Front" so long called for by the Russians became a reality on June 6, 1944. It was my father's birthday, "truly D-day" as he was wont to say, and a marvellous present not just for him but for much of what we came to call "the free world".

There had, it is true, been signs and portents. The aircraft we were seeing flying overhead now had three broad white stripes painted over the camouflage on the wings to allow of prompt identification. There were stories of people on the South coast of England seeming just to disappear for no good reason. It turned out later that they had unwittingly wandered into an area set aside for the hidden and enormous battle resources awaiting the order to invade France. The need for absolute security demanded that they were immediately apprehended and kept there until the invasion was under way lest they break, even unwittingly, the very tight security.

We had been aware that planning for a "second front" had been going on for perhaps more than a year - ever since there was a BBC broadcast asking every citizen to scour his or her attic and chests of drawers to find and send in to Supreme Allied Command in London any holiday postcards or other snaps or pictures, photographs or paintings and sketches of "any part of the world". It had to be put that way, but in fact what the planners in the Inter-Services Topographical Unit wanted was really anything that would allow them to build up maps and photographic records of parts of France most involved in any invasion plans.

Only 24 hours after that broadcast, that military team had a frantic call from the BBC to say that Broadcasting House was rapidly disappearing under a hail of cards and photographs. Thirty thousand had arrived by the first post after the broadcast and the project produced over 10,000,000 pictures. One record states that 50 American servicewomen had to be hastily shipped across the Atlantic simply to collate and classify this enormous response.

Operation "Overlord", as the invasion of France was designated, began just after midnight on 6 June 1944. At home we heard of it first through a bare Communique from the War Office on the early morning BBC News. I remember my father saying to my mother at the breakfast table, "Well, it's started - God help our lads and their Allies!" More adult, he was aware of the risks of not achieving the initial beachhead, and the potential cost in lives of the struggle to do so.

As boys, we were simply thrilled by the great adventure of it all. The school was abuzz with talk before classes and most of us could not suppress our excitement enough to attend to our lessons. We guessed that the teachers too were hard put to contain both their excitement and their curiosity and not to sneak off to the staffroom to hear what news might be coming in by the hour. However, they assumed looks and manners of stern discipline and put us through the hoops as usual.

The practicalities of life were still tough for us then even though we could grasp the fact that the war might come to an end, perhaps within the year. The activity out at the aerodrome was encouraging and did give us a sense of involvement, but the reality that those of us, just a year or two too young, would have to remain mere observers of rather than participants in the struggle was beginning to percolate into our brains. As a result, our play and activity pattern swung from the explicitly warlike preparations of the previous four years or so to more normal teenage preoccupations with playing for the school football team, biking out the road to Portsoy to meet some of the girls at the back of the tennis pavilion there and getting October jobs at the "tatties". After all, we needed the money to pay for our fags. The bonanza of quietly filched cigarettes from my father's study drawer was beginning to dry up because we had fewer military friends about the house, and I was beginning to think he suspected our new-found addiction to the weed.

If the only "picking" we had done in the early years of the war was sphagnum moss in 1939/40, most of us spent two weeks every year thereafter helping with the potato harvest at nearby farms. My mother was chary of releasing me into the community too early (though I never found out whether that was because she thought I was not ready for it, or because she thought it was not ready for me).

Suffice it to say that from about 1943 onwards I spent the two weeks statutory school "Tattie" holiday in October bending my back, along with a miscellany of kids from my own and other areas, trying to keep up with the malevolent rotary digger which flung the potatoes in your

The author, proud of his wartime "black bicycle" outside the Manse at Banff about 1944. These were heavy and unembellished but strongly made.

teeth and past your head as it reached the new ridge of undug spuds before you had even finished collecting those from the present furrow. Hitler came to be seen as a genial and relaxed philanthrope compared to the grieve who spurred us to better and faster efforts for our few bob a day. And dare you miss a few of the wretched spherical roots that might have been half buried in the mire! A mouthful of well chosen AngloSaxon phrases reminded you of your obligations to your employer.

How we prayed for real rain, not just the kind that gently grew a lightly jewelled smirr of dew on your hair or eyebrows. Work was not stopped for that! What we beseeched in our orisons was a proper Ararat-engulfing deluge, a real soaker which would bog down the digger, the tractor, - and the grieve, and afford us a blessed couple of hours lolling in the hayloft, preferably with some of the girls, until it was dry enough for us to start earning our pennies again. Backs were stiff and sore for the first couple of days (from the tattie picking, not the girls in the hayloft) but the work earned us something to help pay for the bike and perhaps a new jacket (if we had the ration coupons).

FINALE

It was not my impression that any of us were driven to the work by sheer patriotism or the memory of "Dig For Victory" posters in the school corridors. What took us to Mill of Boyndie, Paddocklaw or Sandyhills farms was more likely to be peer pressure, "Are ye gan tae the tatties, Davie?," intoned in such a way that you were left in no doubt that the inference was that you were a bit of a softie if you weren't, and of course, money and sex came into it too! The good bits were dinner time at the farm house (11:30 till 12:30) when first we all assembled in the farm kitchen where the farmer's wife then plied us with huge plates of steaming, freshly made broth or other kind of soup with several boiled tatties in it, oatcakes and butter and a cup of tea. The portions were generous and far outdid anything we could have received at home based on our ration book. Then, revived, we would adjourn to the outbuildings or stackyard either to snooze our aches away or engage in other pursuits as opportunity allowed.

These exploits were my first experience of hard physical graft other than digging the garden, for very much shorter periods, but they gave me an understanding of what labour was all about. In a way it was a challenge too and I "got in the way of it", as they say. For years after the war ended I found work at a local farm in the spring and summer when I was a university student and enjoyed the fitness it created in me, the cameraderie with a different group of people who could teach me about the unremitting battle with the land and the elements, rather than the political and national battles that had preoccupied us all in the preceeding years. In short, it did me good.

It also played a large part in stopping my smoking habit. The cattleman at Mill o' Boyndie, watching me puff at a fag while I picked the spuds one day offered me "a real smoke" - a fill of Bogie Roll in a borrowed pipe! If there are those who would still wish to kick the habit, I can recommend smoking that heavy mixture in a short pipe while continually bending over a drill or two of potatoes. It's not really nausea that supervenes - it's closer to death! The episode didn't stop me there and then, but it laid a foundation on which a somewhat healthier lifestyle was later built.

It was a feature of our lives in these later days of the war that

111

we tended to live our lives in little encapsulated chunks. There was the "school" chunk, the "home" chunk, the "work" chunk and the "war" chunk. In each of these we probably operated with somewhat different styles and frames of reference without really being aware of it at the time. It was not hard to immerse oneself in any one of these as required and to shut out the "personae", the other aspects of ourselves, who had peopled the other segments of our lives. The first two of these "chunks" were by far the most secure and patterns of behaviour were very firmly laid down. The work scene was less structured and more open, especially as we grew older; and of course the war scene was part observation and part fantasy. And yet all had to be reconciled even if many of us would have afforded these elements different weightings.

School was, for me, important beyond the others largely because of the importance my family seemed to place on it. I had no close relations, only uncles and cousins actually fighting in the war. Only two of them were killed. But for children whose fathers were away on active service it was a different matter. Then, for them, the war chunk preoccupied them a bit more as the invasion of Europe progressed. The irony of being killed on the last day of the war made those kids' anxiety about their Dads and brothers greater as the days passed by. The routines imposed by school and work helped to distract from these more corrosive thoughts.

Over the weeks that followed the establishment of the beachhead in Normandy, we sensed that after the fall of Caen and the breakout through the Falaise gap the Allies were likely to begin to scent victory. It was a heady brew to sup after so many years of deprivation, "angst" and, for many, loss. There would be those to whom loss had yet to come and as the turn of the year arrived and our armies marched ever closer to the Rhine and the Russians advanced on Berlin, it seemed even more poignant that young men would fall so near the end of this terrible war.

Right to the end the curtain did not come down exactly on the hour the official surrender was achieved on May 8 1945. Even from the airfield at RAF Banff some operational flights were sent out for a few days beyond that, some to escort the King of Norway and his party back to his own land on a RN ship and some to fly patrols along the Norwegian coast lest a few U-boats and other enemy units were unaware that the war had ended.

Even in early 1945 many of us boys became anxious lest the war end before we could taste the glamour and glory (as we saw it) of uniform and action. But, aged 15 and now near the top of the school, I was firmly reminded by my teachers that survival in the brave new post-war world would require effort and qualifications and this was the time to buckle down and suppress our military fantasies.

It had been a long time now since German aircraft had intruded on Scottish airspace. The Battle of the Atlantic had been long since won and as stories began to trickle out of Hitler's last infamous demise at his own hand in his bunker in a defeated Berlin, the first pictures of the emaciated, and in many cases moribund, bodies of the survivors of the Death Camps of Belsen and Auschwitz began to appear in the press. There had, of course, been rumours and patchy evidence of the "Holocaust", as it came to be known, for some years but this awful confirmation of the torture, slaughter and degradation of our fellow men just because they were Jewish offended and saddened all of us who saw it in the press and on Movietone News at the cinemas. Little did I know then that only six years later I would myself come face to face with the gruesome evidence in a forest in Westphalia. But that's another story.

During these last months of the war in Europe we watched the advance through France, the Low Countries and then across the Rhine into Germany itself with a growing confidence that we would live to tell the tale of our boyhood through the war years. All the while, the "forgotten armies" in the far East slogged it out with the Japs in Burma and the Pacific islands. We had seen Germans, albeit wounded or prisoners. They were real enough, and in many ways not unlike ourselves. We had never seen Japs except on the newsreels and the latter always seemed to take good care that we would perceive them as an alien culture, typified by their habits of committing hara-kiri when captured or doing it for the glory of the Rising Sun as Kamikaze pilots diving, sometimes in vain, on battleships or aircraft carriers.

The brainwashing that went on in the war was more

self criticism and fair judgment to develop a new attitude to our former enemies. At the time of writing it is clear that there are those who have not yet succeeded in this. It is perhaps important to realise that we all saw final victory in the war as a goal which would be the prelude to a new and fairer world.

In due course the General Election of 1945 simply confirmed a ground swell of political opinion which the war had fostered. People examining now the practices and policies of the Commanders and the Governments which concurred in the decision to use the atom bomb on the Japanese need to realise that anything then which would bring the war to a quick conclusion and return the men to their homes and families after six harrowing years was more than desirable. Hardly any would have been in a position to consider whether the final surrender of the Japs would have been offered soon regardless of whether the atom bomb had been dropped or not. Those who had seen their men who had served in Europe and the Atlantic gradually returning home to civilian life again simply wanted those in the East to join them as soon as possible.

For myself, when VE (Victory in Europe) Day dawned on May 8, 1945, my feelings were not of unequivocal rejoicing. Certainly the school had been given a holiday and there were bonfires, a ceremonial tearing down of blackout curtains, tape off the windows and, for once, the street lights suddenly making night into day (though in the north, in May, we had to wait up very late to see the full effect). Even the "black hole" under the stair had the bunk moved out, the torches and candles reverted to peacetime uses and it became the repository of the cleaning materials and brushes it had originally been. But my dreams of challenging the Nazis in airforce blue had suddenly been shattered and even the consolation of knowing that the Japs might hang on for a bit longer was not enough to convince me that the more boring target of sitting my "Highers" at school would come well before any sallies into the armed Services.

Then, on August 9, 1945, a B17 of the USAAF dropped "Fat Man", the second atomic bomb, on Nagasaki. The first, "Little Boy", (you could bet they'd both be "male"!) had been dropped on Hiroshima, with devastating results, only three days before. Seeing the photographs and newsreel of the results soon after was awesome even to us, the victors. There was a feeling that we had entered a new era. The tail gunner of the aircraft which dropped it said later that he had "had a peep into Hell".

So it happened that on August 15, the final unconditional surrender of Japan was broadcast and all hostilities ceased. Wives, mothers and sisters prepared to welcome back their men. We hung a Union Jack out of the bedroom window and placed V for Victory signs in the others. My father and mother celebrated with a sherry. Even Tom and I were allowed a small one that evening before my father closeted himself in his study to write his Thanksgiving sermon for Sunday. My war had ended.

Bibliography

Calder, A (1969)   **"The People's War":**
Jonathan Cape : London.

FitzGibbon, C (1957) **"The Blitz":**
Allan Wingate : London.

Hughes, J (1991)   **"A Steep Turn to the Stars"** :
Benevenagh Books : Elgin

Longmate,N (1971) **"How We Lived Then"** :
Arrow : London.

Smith, D J (1989)   **"Action Stations" (Vol. 7)** :
Thorson's : Wellingborough.